North Carolina Guardianship Manual

2008

John L. Saxon

North Carolina Indigent Defense Manual Series
John Rubin, Editor

UNC
SCHOOL OF GOVERNMENT

north carolina
indigent defense
manual series

Production of this series is made possible by funding
from the North Carolina Office of Indigent Defense Services.

The School of Government at the University of North Carolina at Chapel Hill works to improve the lives of North Carolinians by engaging in practical scholarship that helps public officials and citizens understand and strengthen state and local government. Established in 1931 as the Institute of Government, the School provides educational, advisory, and research services for state and local governments. The School of Government is also home to a nationally ranked graduate program in public administration and specialized centers focused on information technology, environmental finance, and civic education for youth.

As the largest university-based local government training, advisory, and research organization in the United States, the School of Government offers up to 200 classes, seminars, schools, and specialized conferences for more than 12,000 public officials each year. In addition, faculty members annually publish approximately fifty books, periodicals, and other reference works related to state and local government. Each day that the General Assembly is in session, the School produces the Daily Bulletin, which reports on the day's activities for members of the legislature and others who need to follow the course of legislation.

The Master of Public Administration Program is a full-time, two-year program that serves up to sixty students annually. It consistently ranks among the best public administration graduate programs in the country, particularly in city management. With courses ranging from public policy analysis to ethics and management, the program educates leaders for local, state, and federal governments and nonprofit organizations.

Operating support for the School of Government's programs and activities comes from many sources, including state appropriations, local government membership dues, private contributions, publication sales, course fees, and service contracts. Visit www.sog.unc.edu or call 919.966.5381 for more information on the School's courses, publications, programs, and services.

Michael R. Smith, DEAN
Thomas H. Thornburg, SENIOR ASSOCIATE DEAN
Frayda S. Bluestein, ASSOCIATE DEAN FOR PROGRAMS
Todd A. Nicolet, ASSOCIATE DEAN FOR INFORMATION TECHNOLOGY
Ann Cary Simpson, ASSOCIATE DEAN FOR DEVELOPMENT AND COMMUNICATIONS
Bradley G. Volk, ASSOCIATE DEAN FOR ADMINISTRATION

FACULTY

Gregory S. Allison
Stephen Allred (on leave)
David N. Ammons
A. Fleming Bell, II
Maureen M. Berner
Mark F. Botts
Joan G. Brannon
Molly C. Broad
Michael Crowell
Shea Riggsbee Denning
James C. Drennan
Richard D. Ducker
Robert L. Farb
Joseph S. Ferrell
Milton S. Heath Jr.
Norma Houston (on leave)

Cheryl Daniels Howell
Joseph E. Hunt
Willow S. Jacobson
Robert P. Joyce
Diane M. Juffras
David M. Lawrence
Dona G. Lewandowski
James M. Markham
Janet Mason
Laurie L. Mesibov
Kara A. Millonzi
Jill D. Moore
Jonathan Q. Morgan
Ricardo S. Morse
David W. Owens
William C. Rivenbark

Dale J. Roenigk
John Rubin
John L. Saxon
Shannon H. Schelin
Jessica Smith
Karl W. Smith
Carl W. Stenberg III
John B. Stephens
Charles Szypszak
Vaughn Upshaw
A. John Vogt
Aimee N. Wall
Richard B. Whisnant
Gordon P. Whitaker
Eileen Youens

ISBN 978-1-56011-580-9

ABOUT THE NORTH CAROLINA INDIGENT DEFENSE MANUAL SERIES

The North Carolina Indigent Defense Manual Series is a collection of reference manuals addressing law and practice in areas in which indigent defendants and respondents are entitled to the representation of counsel at state expense. The series was created to address the need for comprehensive, up-to-date reference materials for public defenders and appointed counsel, who devote their time, skill, and effort to representing poor people. In addition to assisting indigent defenders with their responsibilities, the manuals also may be useful to others who work in the court system and who need a reference source on the law. In keeping with the School of Government's commitment to practical scholarship, the manuals are written by authors with subject-matter expertise in their respective fields, experience in developing effective educational materials, and knowledge of how things actually work in practice. The editor of the series is John Rubin, a member of the School of Government faculty who specializes in indigent defense education. For a current listing of manuals in the series, see www.indigentdefense.unc.edu. Production of the series is made possible by funding from the North Carolina Office of Indigent Defense Services, which is responsible for overseeing and enhancing the provision of indigent defense representation in North Carolina.

ABOUT THE AUTHOR OF THE NORTH CAROLINA GUARDIANSHIP MANUAL

John L. Saxon is a Professor of Public Law and Government at the School of Government. He joined the faculty in 1992, and his areas of interest include social services law, child support, elder law, and family policy. Prior to this appointment, he worked for 15 years as an attorney for the U.S. Senate and the U.S. Department of the Interior, and as a legal services lawyer in South Carolina, Virginia, and North Carolina. He is the editor of *North Carolina Legislation 1997* and *North Carolina Legislation 1998*, is co-author of *The Law and the Elderly in North Carolina*, and has written numerous articles and bulletins on welfare reform, social services, child support, and elder law.

Table of Contents

Preface

In 2007, the N.C. Office of Indigent Defense Services asked the UNC-Chapel Hill School of Government to develop a training program for attorneys who are appointed pursuant to G.S. 35A-1107 to represent allegedly incapacitated adults in guardianship proceedings.

Recognizing that there was no comprehensive treatise or practice manual on the subject of North Carolina guardianship law, I offered to write a *North Carolina Guardianship Manual* that would serve as a training and reference resource for attorneys who are appointed to represent incapacitated adults in guardianship proceedings. As such, it is part of a series of manuals produced by the School of Government on indigent defense practice areas, including the *North Carolina Defender Manual* and the *North Carolina Civil Commitment Manual* (2006).

It is important to note that this manual does not address all aspects of North Carolina's guardianship law. It does not, for example, address most of the issues that arise in an adult guardianship proceeding following the appointment of a guardian for an incapacitated adult. Nor does it address in detail the powers and duties of guardians or the appointment of guardians for minors. Instead, it focuses almost exclusively on those aspects of adult guardianship matters in which attorneys who are appointed under G.S. 35A-1107 are involved—especially proceedings to determine whether an adult is incapacitated, proceedings to appoint a guardian for an incapacitated adult, and proceedings seeking the restoration of a ward's incapacity.

Despite this, however, I hope that this manual will be of value to others who are involved in adult guardianship proceedings, including Clerks of Superior Court, superior court judges, lawyers who are retained to represent petitioners or respondents in adult guardianship proceedings, and public agencies (such as county social services departments) that may be involved in adult guardianship proceedings.

In writing this manual, I have made the conscious decision to use the terms "capacity," "incapacity," and "incapacitated," rather than "competency," "incompetency," and "incompetent," whenever possible and appropriate. It is true that North Carolina's guardianship statute (Chapter 35A of the General Statutes) still uses "incompetent" and similar terms. I feel, however, that those terms are antiquated, pejorative, and inaccurate, and that the term "incapacitated" is preferable. It is important to note, though, that the use of "incapacitated" in this manual relates only to questions of capacity in connection with adult guardianship proceedings under G.S. Chapter 35A and does not apply to other legal proceedings, such as criminal proceedings or involuntary commitment proceedings, in which the issue of capacity may arise.

No book is ever solely the product of its author, and this manual is no exception. In writing this manual, I received much assistance and support from many people. My colleagues on the faculty at the School of Government, John Rubin, Janet Mason, Joan Brannon, and Ann Anderson, reviewed the entire manuscript and offered many valuable suggestions and corrections, as did several other reviewers, including Dolly Whiteside (Special Counsel Supervising Attorney, N.C. Office of Indigent Defense Services), Pamela Weaver Best (Deputy Legal Counsel, N.C. Administrative Office of the Courts), Ben N. Turnage (Special Counsel, N.C. Office of Indigent Defense Services), and Patricia Kay Gibbons, Esq. (Raleigh, NC). I would also like to note my special appreciation to the American Psychological Association and the American Bar Association's Commission on Law and Aging for their permission to include the copyrighted materials that appear in the appendices to Chapter 6. I also want to thank Robby Poore, Kevin Justice, Sarah McConnaghy, Katrina Hunt, Chris Toenes, and Angela Williams of the Publications Division of the School of Government for their assistance in producing this manual.

Although I hope that the information included in this manual is entirely accurate, I realize that it may include some mistakes or errors (as well as perspectives and legal opinions with which some may disagree) and invite readers to contact me (saxon@sog.unc.edu or 919-966-4289) if they feel there is anything in the manual that is not correct or needs to be changed, added, or deleted in the next edition of this manual.

John L. Saxon
Professor of Public Law and Government
School of Government
The University of North Carolina at Chapel Hill
Chapel Hill, North Carolina

January 2008

CHAPTER 1:
Overview of Adult Guardianship

1.1
Scope of this Manual

This manual is written for attorneys who are appointed to represent allegedly incapacitated adults in proceedings to appoint general guardians, guardians of the person, or guardians of the estate for those adults under Articles 1, 2, 4, and 5 of G.S. Chapter 35A.

This manual focuses primarily on the law and procedure governing proceedings to determine whether a person is an incapacitated adult, to appoint a guardian for an incapacitated adult, and to "restore" the competency of an incapacitated adult. It does not discuss in detail many other aspects of guardianship law, such as the powers and duties of guardians, guardianship bonds, accountings, and removal of guardians because those matters generally do not fall within the scope of representation by attorneys who are appointed in guardianship proceedings under G.S. 35A-1107.

Similarly, because attorneys are not appointed to represent minors who are the subjects of guardianship proceedings under Article 6 of G.S. Chapter 35A, this manual does not address in detail the law governing the appointment of guardians for minors (other than those who are at least 17 ½ years old and are alleged to be incapacitated for reasons other than their minority).

1.2
Scope of this Chapter

This chapter introduces readers to the terminology of guardianship and provides a general overview of the law of adult guardianship generally and legal proceedings to appoint guardians for incapacitated adults. Detailed information regarding legal proceedings to appoint guardians for incapacitated adults is provided in the remaining chapters of this manual.

Readers are encouraged to familiarize themselves with the guardianship terminology in the following section of this chapter before reading the rest of this chapter and the remaining chapters of the manual.

1.3
Adult Guardianship Terminology

Accounting. The process by which the guardian files with the Clerk of Superior Court for the Clerk's review and approval financial reports and information concerning the ward's property, estate, and financial affairs, including the receipt and expenditure of the ward's money and transactions involving the ward's property. *See* G.S. Ch. 35A, Art. 10.

Adult. A person who is at least 18 years of age or who is under the age of 18 and has been legally emancipated. A minor who is at least 17 ½ years old is treated like an adult for purposes of a guardianship proceeding if the minor is incapacitated due to reasons other than his or her minority. *See* G.S. 35A-1101(8).

Adult guardianship. Procedures involving the appointment of a guardian for an incapacitated adult (as opposed to proceedings involving the appointment of a guardian for a minor).

Ancillary guardian. A guardian of the estate who is appointed pursuant to G.S. 35A-1280 on behalf of a nonresident ward when a general guardian, guardian of the estate, or similar fiduciary has been appointed for the ward under the laws of another state and the ward has an ownership or other interest in real or personal property in North Carolina.

Applicant. Any person, including any state or local human services agency, who files an application seeking the appointment of a guardian for an incapacitated adult. *See* G.S. 35A-1210. In most adult guardianship proceedings, the petitioner is also the only applicant. However, a person other than the petitioner may be the only or an additional applicant in some adult guardianship proceedings.

Clerk. The Clerk of Superior Court. The Clerk has original jurisdiction over guardianship proceedings and exclusive, original jurisdiction except in cases in which the Clerk has a direct or indirect interest. The Clerk's judicial authority may be exercised by an Assistant Clerk of Superior Court.

Corporate guardian. A for-profit or nonprofit corporation whose corporate charter expressly authorizes it to serve as a guardian or in a similar fiduciary capacity. *See* G.S. 35A-1213(c).

Court. The Clerk of Superior Court or a Superior Court Judge. The Clerk has original jurisdiction over guardianship proceedings and exclusive, original jurisdiction except in cases in which the Clerk has a direct or indirect interest. Except as noted above, judges of the Superior Court exercise appellate, rather than original, jurisdiction over guardianship proceedings.

Designated human services agency. A state or local human services agency (including a state, county, city, area, or regional social services agency, public health agency, mental health agency, mental retardation or developmental disability agency, substance abuse agency, vocational rehabilitation agency, aging agency, or diagnostic evaluation agency or center) that is designated by the court to submit a multidisciplinary evaluation in an adult guardianship proceeding or to review status reports regarding an incapacitated ward. *See* G.S. 35A-1101(4); G.S. 35A-1101(14); G.S. 35A-1111; G.S. 35A-1202(3); G.S. 35A-1212(b); G.S. 35A-1242.

Disinterested public agent guardian. The director or assistant director of a local human services (social services, public health, mental health, aging, etc.) agency or an officer, agent, or employee of a state human services agency who is appointed by the Clerk of Court to serve as the guardian of an incapacitated ward. *See* G.S. 35A-1202(4); G.S. 35A-1213(d); G.S. 35A-1213(e).

Durable power of attorney. A valid power of attorney executed pursuant to G.S. Ch. 32A, Art. 2, or a similar statute of another state, under which the attorney-in-fact's authority is not affected by the principal's subsequent mental incapacity. *See* G.S. 32A-8; G.S. 32A-10.

Estate. Any interest, including any interest in joint accounts or jointly-held property, of the ward in real property, choses in action, intangible personal property, and tangible personal property. G.S. 35A-1202(5).

General guardian. A guardian who has the authority of a guardian of the person and a guardian of the estate of an incapacitated ward. G.S. 35A-1202(7).

Guardian. A general guardian, guardian of the person, guardian of the estate, or interim guardian of an incapacitated adult.

Guardian ad litem. When used in the context of guardianship proceedings under G.S. Chapter 35A, guardian ad litem means an attorney who is appointed pursuant to G.S. 35A-1107 to represent or serve as the guardian ad litem for an allegedly incapacitated respondent or an incapacitated ward in a proceeding to determine the respondent's or ward's capacity or to appoint a guardian for the respondent. When used in other contexts, guardian ad litem refers to a person who is appointed pursuant to Rule 17 of the North Carolina Rules of Civil Procedure as the guardian ad litem for an incompetent person who is a party to a civil action or proceeding. *See* G.S. 35A-1101(6); G.S. 35A-1202(8).

Guardian of the estate. A guardian who is appointed solely for the purpose of managing the property, estate, and business affairs of an incapacitated ward. G.S. 35A-1202(9). *See also* G.S. 35A-1251; G.S. 35A-1253. In some states, a guardian of the estate is referred to as a "conservator."

Guardian of the person. A guardian who is appointed solely for the purpose of performing duties relating to the care, custody, and control of an incapacitated ward. G.S. 35A-1202(10). *See also* G.S. 35A-1241.

Guardianship. A legal relationship under which a person or agency (the guardian) is appointed by a court to make decisions and act on behalf of a minor or an incapacitated adult (the ward) with respect to the ward's personal affairs, financial affairs, or both.

Health care power of attorney. A valid health care power of attorney that is executed pursuant to G.S. Ch. 32A, Art. 3, or a similar law of another state, under which a health care agent is authorized to make health care decisions on behalf of the principal when the principal lacks capacity to make or communicate health care decisions. *See* G.S. 32A-19; G.S. 32A-20; G.S. 32A-22.

Incapacitated (or incompetent). Lacking sufficient mental capacity to manage one's own personal affairs, financial affairs, or property or lacking sufficient mental or physical capacity to make or communicate important decisions concerning one's own person, family, or property due to mental illness, mental retardation or developmental disability, inebriety, disease, injury, or similar cause or condition. G.S. 35A-1101(1); G.S. 35A-1101(2); G.S. 35A-1101(5); G.S. 35A-1101(7); G.S. 35A-1101(10); G.S. 35A-1101(12); G.S. 35A-1101(13).

Note: Although North Carolina's guardianship statutes use the term "incompetent," this manual will use the term "incapacitated" instead of "incompetent."

Incapacitated (or incompetent) adult. An incapacitated person who is at least 18 years old or who is a minor who is at least 17½ years old and, apart from his or her status as a minor, is incapacitated. G.S. 35A-1101(7); G.S. 35A-1101(8).

Interim guardian. A temporary guardian who is appointed pursuant to G.S. 35A-1114 for a respondent who is alleged to be incapacitated in order to protect the respondent's well-being or estate from imminent harm. G.S. 35A-1101(11).

Letters of appointment. The document issued by the Clerk of Superior Court to a general guardian, guardian of the person, or guardian of the estate, following the guardian's appointment and qualification, authorizing the guardian to act as the ward's guardian. *See* G.S. 35A-1206.

Limited guardianship. A guardianship in which the guardianship order expressly limits the guardian's powers or permits an incapacitated ward to retain certain legal rights or privileges that are within the ward's comprehension and judgment. *See* G.S. 35A-1215(b).

Minor. A person who is under the age of 18 years and is not emancipated.

Multidisciplinary evaluation (MDE). An evaluation that is prepared by a designated human services agency at the direction of the Clerk of Superior Court regarding the nature and extent of a respondent's or ward's incapacity in order to assist the Clerk in determining whether or to what extent the respondent is incapacitated, whether a limited guardianship is appropriate, or other issues regarding guardianship. An MDE must include current (within the past year) medical, psychological, and social work evaluations as directed by the Clerk and may include evaluations by other professionals regarding the respondent's or ward's needs with respect to education, vocational rehabilitation, occupational therapy, vocational therapy, psychiatry, speech therapy, etc. G.S. 35A-1101(14); G.S. 35A-1111; G.S. 35A-1202(13); G.S. 35A-1212(b).

Natural guardian. The parent of a minor child.

Practice Note: An incapacitated adult does not have a natural guardian.

Nominated guardian. A person who has been nominated by a competent adult, pursuant to a duly executed durable power of attorney, health care power of attorney, or other writing, to serve as the adult's guardian in the event that the adult is determined to be incapacitated and in need of a guardian.

Nonresident guardian. A guardian who is not a resident of North Carolina. *See* G.S. 35A-1213(b).

Petitioner. Any person, including any state or local human services agency, who files a petition alleging that a respondent is incapacitated and needs a guardian. *See* G.S. 35A-1105. In most adult guardianship proceedings, the petitioner is also the applicant who seeks the appointment of a guardian for an incapacitated adult. *See* G.S. 35A-1210.

Plenary guardianship. An adult guardianship in which the guardianship order does not limit the guardian's statutory powers or permit the ward to retain specified legal rights or privileges.

Public guardian. A person appointed by the Clerk of Superior Court pursuant to G.S. Ch. 35A, Art. 11, to serve as the guardian of an incapacitated adult when (a) the incapacitated adult does not have a guardian and six months have elapsed since the discovery of property belonging to the incapacitated adult, or (b) any person who is entitled to letters of guardianship with respect to an incapacitated adult requests the Clerk to issue letters of appointment to the public guardian.

Representative payee. A person or agency who has been designated by the Social Security Administration or another federal or state agency to receive and use public benefits, such as Social Security, Supplemental Security Income, or veterans' benefits, on behalf of and for the benefit of a beneficiary who has been determined to be unable to manage the benefits or assistance to which he or she is entitled.

Respondent. The person who is alleged to be incapacitated in an adult guardianship proceeding under G.S. Ch. 35A. G.S. 35A-1101(15). If a respondent is adjudicated incapacitated and a guardian is appointed for the respondent, the respondent generally is referred to thereafter as the ward. *See* G.S. 35A-1101(17); G.S. 35A-1202(15).

Standby guardian. A person who has been designated or appointed pursuant to G.S. Ch. 35A, Art. 21, to become the guardian of a minor child upon the death or incapacity of the child's parent.

Practice Note: North Carolina law currently does not provide for the designation or appointment of a standby guardian for an incapacitated adult.

Status report. A report filed pursuant to G.S. 35A-1242 by a general guardian or guardian of the person regarding an incapacitated ward's condition, needs, and development and the guardian's performance of his or her duties.

Substituted judgment. A decision-making standard under which a guardian considers the ward's known preferences, attitudes, beliefs, wishes, etc., in an attempt to make the same decision for a ward that the ward would have made if the ward had the capacity to make the decision.

Successor guardian. A guardian who is appointed following the death, resignation, or removal of a guardian.

Testamentary guardian. A person who is nominated by the last will and testament of the parent of a minor child pursuant to G.S. 35A-1225 to become the minor child's guardian upon the parent's death.

Practice Note: The provisions of G.S. 35A-1225 do not apply to incapacitated adults.

Ward. An incapacitated adult for whom a guardian has been appointed in an adult guardianship proceeding. G.S. 35A-1101(17); 35A-1202(15).

1.4
Nature and Purpose of Adult Guardianship

A. Definition of Guardianship

Guardianship is a legal relationship under which a person or agency (the guardian) is appointed by a court to make decisions and act on behalf of a minor or an incapacitated adult (the ward) with respect to the ward's personal affairs, financial affairs, or both.

B. Purpose of Guardianship

The essential purpose of guardianship for an incapacitated adult is to replace, in whole or in part, the ward's authority to make personal decisions with the guardian's authority to make decisions regarding the ward's personal affairs, financial affairs, or both when the ward lacks sufficient mental capacity to make those decisions. *See* G.S. 35A-1201(a)(3). Guardianship, however, should seek to preserve for an incapacitated ward the opportunity to make those decisions and exercise those rights that are within the ward's comprehension and judgment, allowing for the possibility of error to the same degree as is allowed to competent adults. G.S. 35A-1201(a)(5). And even when a guardian has been appointed for an incapacitated ward, the ward should be allowed to participate, to the maximum extent of his or her capabilities, in all decisions that will affect him or her. G.S. 35A-1201(a)(5).

C. Personal Autonomy

The concepts of personal autonomy and self-determination hold that all "competent" adults have, or should have, the right to make their own decisions regarding their personal affairs. These concepts, in turn, rest on at least two assumptions:

- absent a contrary and legitimate social or governmental interest, "competent" adults should be free to make their own decisions regarding their personal affairs;

- absent proof that an adult lacks sufficient mental capacity to make personal decisions, an adult has the capacity to make his or her own decisions.

Both of these assumptions are recognized, explicitly or implicitly, by the common law, case law, statutory law, and constitutional law.

The United States Supreme Court has held that a competent adult has a constitutionally-protected, but not absolute, interest in making certain types of important, intimate, or personal decisions, including decisions regarding the refusal of medical treatment. *Cruzan v. Missouri Dept. of Health*, 497 U.S. 261, 278 (1990); *cf. Washington v. Glucksberg*, 521 U.S. 702 (1997). *See also Hagins v. Greensboro Redevelopment Comm'n*, 275 N.C. 90, 106 (1969) (holding that the government may not interfere with a competent adult's authority to make decisions regarding his or her person or property absent actual and positive necessity therefor).

D. Presumption of Capacity

The law also presumes that, in the absence of proof to the contrary, all adults have sufficient mental capacity to make their own decisions regarding their personal affairs. *See State v. Thompson*, 328 N.C. 477 (1991); *Ridings v. Ridings*, 55 N.C. App. 630 (1982); *In re Womack*, 53 N.C. App. 221 (1981); *State v. Jones*, 293 N.C. 413 (1977); *Hagins v. Greensboro Redevelopment Comm'n*, 275 N.C. 90 (1969) (presumption implicit in holding); *Jones v. Winstead*, 186 N.C. 536 (1923); *Hudson v. Hudson*, 144 N.C. 449 (1907).

This presumption, however, may be rebutted by sufficient, competent evidence of mental incapacity in a legal proceeding, including a guardianship proceeding pursuant to G.S. Ch. 35A, in which an adult's mental capacity is at issue.

E. Balancing Personal Autonomy vs. Protection of Incapacitated Persons

Guardianship necessarily limits the personal autonomy and legal rights of an incapacitated ward. Guardianship, however, also may protect an incapacitated person or his or her property. The law of guardianship, therefore, reflects an attempt to strike a balance between preserving and protecting the legal rights, freedom, and personal autonomy of adults and the duty of the State (acting as *parens patriae*) to protect individuals who lack sufficient mental capacity to make decisions regarding themselves or their property, to act in their own best interests, or to protect themselves or their property from harm, injury, or exploitation.

One of the ways that the law attempts to balance the competing interests of personal autonomy and protection of incapacitated persons is by defining the conditions that will warrant the State's limiting an adult's legal rights through the appointment of a guardian to make decisions and act for that adult. Legal definitions of "incapacity" or "incompetence," along with legal concepts regarding "limited guardianship," "least restrictive" alternative, "last resort," or "necessity," constitute the legal "triggers" that justify limiting an adult's legal rights through the appointment of a guardian.

Unlike the Uniform Guardianship and Protective Proceedings Act, North Carolina's guardianship statutes do not expressly provide that a guardian may be appointed for an incapacitated adult only if there are no "less restrictive" alternatives that will meet the adult's needs. North Carolina law, however, does provide that limiting the rights of an incapacitated adult through the appointment of a guardian should not be undertaken unless it is clear that guardianship will give the ward a fuller capacity for exercising his or her rights. G.S. 35A-1201(a)(4).

North Carolina's guardianship statutes also implicitly encourage the use of "limited guardianships" and expressly allow the entry of "limited guardianship" orders under which the ward retains specified legal rights. G.S. 35A-1215(b).

A second way in which the law attempts to balance the competing interests of autonomy and protection is by establishing the legal procedures that govern the determination of incapacity and the appointment of a guardian for an incapacitated adult. At a minimum, these procedures must provide an allegedly incapacitated adult with adequate notice and a fair opportunity to be heard before he or she is determined to be mentally incapacitated and a guardian is appointed for him or her. *See Hagins v. Greensboro Redevelopment Comm'n*, 275 N.C. 90 (1969).

F. The Guardian-Ward Relationship

Guardianship involves a fiduciary relationship between the guardian and the ward. The general guardian or guardian of the estate of an incapacitated ward has a fiduciary obligation to manage the ward's estate reasonably, prudently, and in the ward's best interest. *See* G.S. 35A-1253; *In re Armfield*, 113 N.C. App. 467 (1994); *Cline v. Teich*, 92 N.C. App. 257 (1988); *Kuykendall v. Proctor*, 270 N.C. 510 (1967); *State ex rel. Armfield v. Brown*, 73 N.C. 81 (1875). Similarly, a general guardian or guardian of the person of an incapacitated ward is required to act in good faith and in the ward's best interest. *See* G.S. 35A-1241.

1.5
Guardianship Law in North Carolina

Most of North Carolina's statutory law regarding incapacity and guardianship is codified in G.S. Ch. 35A. There is only a limited amount of North Carolina case law regarding guardianship, and most of that case law predates the 1977 and 1987 guardianship legislation described below.

A. Guardianship Law Before 1977

American guardianship statutes find their origin in a 1324 English statute under which the Lord Chancellor, acting on behalf of the King, was authorized to appoint a committee for the person and property of "idiots" and "lunatics."

North Carolina's first statute regarding guardianship was enacted in 1784, authorizing the county courts to appoint guardians for "idiots and lunatics." In 1868, jurisdiction with respect to guardianship proceedings was transferred to the Clerk of Superior Court.

Before 1977, North Carolina's guardianship law contained few provisions protecting the due process rights of allegedly incapacitated respondents and focused primarily on the investment, management, use, and sale of the property of minor and incapacitated wards.

B. The 1977 Amendments to G.S. Chapter 35

In 1977, the General Assembly enacted legislation
- replacing pejorative language ("idiot," "lunatic," "feeble-minded," "insane," etc.) in North Carolina's guardianship statutes with the term "incompetent adult,"
- providing due process protections for allegedly incompetent respondents,
- introducing the concept of "limited guardianship,"
- allowing the court to order a "multidisciplinary evaluation" of an allegedly incompetent respondent,
- allowing the appointment of interim guardians in cases of emergency,

- allowing the appointment of state and local human services directors and employees as "disinterested public agent" guardians,
- defining the powers and duties of guardians of the person, and
- requiring certain guardians to file "status reports" regarding their wards with the court.

The 1977 legislation, however, applied primarily with respect to persons who were incompetent or allegedly incompetent due to mental retardation, epilepsy, cerebral palsy, or autism and did not significantly affect respondents and wards whose incapacity or alleged incapacity was due to mental illness, "senility," inebriety, or other causes.

C. The 1987 Enactment of G.S. Chapter 35A

In 1987, the General Assembly enacted G.S. Ch. 35A, consolidated and clarified North Carolina's statutory law governing guardianship of minors and incapacitated adults, and extended the provisions of the 1977 legislation to all allegedly incompetent respondents and incompetent wards.

D. The Uniform Guardianship and Protective Proceedings Act

North Carolina has not enacted the Uniform Guardianship and Protective Proceedings Act (UGPPA).

1.6
Overview of Adult Guardianship Proceedings

This section provides a brief overview of adult guardianship proceedings. Detailed information regarding adult guardianship proceedings is included in the remaining chapters of this manual.

A. Jurisdiction

The Clerk of Superior Court has original jurisdiction over guardianship proceedings involving allegedly incapacitated adults and incapacitated wards. G.S. 35A-1103; G.S. 35A-1203. (The Clerk of Superior Court also has original and exclusive jurisdiction with respect to guardianship proceedings involving minors, other than juveniles who are subject to the jurisdiction of the district court in juvenile proceedings under G.S. Ch. 7B.) The Clerk's jurisdiction over proceedings to appoint a guardian for an incapacitated adult is exclusive, except in cases in which the Clerk has a direct or indirect interest in the proceeding, in which case jurisdiction is vested in any superior court judge residing or presiding in the district in which the proceeding is brought. G.S. 35A-1103(d).

B. Procedure

Proceedings to appoint a guardian for an incapacitated adult are commenced by filing a verified petition with the Clerk of Superior Court. G.S. 35A-1105. Upon the filing of a petition, an attorney must be appointed to represent the respondent. G.S. 35A-1107. Counsel appointed for the respondent may be discharged if the respondent retains counsel. G.S. 35A-1107. Copies of the petition and notice of hearing must be served personally on the respondent. G.S. 35A-1109.

The Clerk may appoint an interim guardian for the respondent before the hearing to determine the respondent's incapacity if the petitioner files a motion seeking the appointment of an interim guardian and the Clerk finds that there is reasonable cause to believe that the respondent is incapacitated and that there is an imminent or foreseeable risk of harm to the respondent's physical well-being that requires immediate intervention or that there is an imminent or foreseeable risk of harm to the respondent's estate that requires immediate intervention in order to protect the respondent's interest. G.S. 35A-1114.

C. Determining Incapacity and Appointing a Guardian

In order to appoint a guardian for an adult respondent, the court (or jury) must find, after hearing and by clear, cogent, and convincing evidence, that the respondent lacks sufficient capacity to manage his or her own affairs or to make or communicate important decisions concerning his or her person, family, or property, due to mental illness, mental retardation, inebriety, disease, injury, or similar cause or condition. G.S. 35A-1101(7); G.S. 35A-1112(d).

The respondent or respondent's attorney may request that the issue of incapacity be determined by a jury. G.S. 35A-1110. If a jury trial is not requested by the respondent or ordered by the court, the issue of incapacity is determined by the court.

If a respondent is adjudicated incapacitated, the Clerk must, after hearing evidence regarding the nature and extent of the needed guardianship, the assets, liabilities, and needs of the ward, and the suitability of prospective guardians, appoint a general guardian, a guardian of the person, or a guardian of the estate for the incapacitated ward. G.S. 35A-1120; G.S. 35A-1212.

The Clerk of Superior Court may order that issues related to the guardianship of an incapacitated adult be referred for mediation. G.S. 7A-38.3B.

D. Qualification, Powers, and Duties of Guardians

To qualify as a guardian, a person or corporation must meet the statutory qualifications for appointment as a guardian and, except in the case of specified guardians of the person who are not disinterested public agent guardians or public guardians, post a bond with the Clerk of Superior Court. After qualifying, general guardians and guardians of the estate are required to file inventories and accountings with the Clerk of Superior Court. Some general guardians and guardians of the person are required to file status reports with the Clerk or a designated human services agency.

Unless otherwise provided by the Clerk, the powers and duties of guardians are those set forth in G.S. Ch. 35A and other applicable statutory or case law. The Clerk may enter a "limited guardianship" order under which the guardian's statutory powers are limited and the ward retains certain rights and privileges. G.S. 35A-1212(a); G.S. 35A-1215(b).

E. Appeal

Appeal from the Clerk's order adjudicating incapacity or appointing a guardian for an incapacitated ward is to the Superior Court. G.S. 35A-1115; G.S. 1-301.2; G.S. 1-301.3. Notice of appeal must be filed within 10 days of the date the Clerk's order is entered. On appeal, the Superior Court hears the case *de novo* with respect to the issue of incapacity but may reverse and remand the Clerk's order regarding appointment of a guardian only if the judge finds that the Clerk's findings were not supported by the evidence in the record before the Clerk, that the Clerk's conclusions of law are not supported by the Clerk's findings, or that the Clerk's order is inconsistent with the Clerk's conclusions of law or with applicable law.

F. Modification and Termination of Guardianship

An incapacitated ward, the ward's guardian, or any interested person may file a motion with the Clerk requesting that the ward's capacity be "restored." G.S. 35A-1130.

The Clerk of Superior Court has jurisdiction to hear motions requesting modification of guardianship orders or any other matter pertaining to a pending guardianship, to remove guardians, and to appoint successor guardians. G.S. 35A-1207; G.S. 35A-1290; G.S. 35A-1293.

The guardianship of an incapacitated ward terminates when the ward dies, when the ward's capacity is restored, or when the Clerk enters an order terminating the guardianship. *See* G.S. 35A-1295.

1.7
Legal Consequences of Guardianship

A. Presumption of Incapacity

The fact that a person has been determined to be incapacitated under G.S. Ch. 35A creates a presumption that he or she lacks mental capacity from the date on which he or she was adjudicated "incompetent," and this presumption is binding against the ward and parties in privity with the ward in other civil actions absent an order "restoring" the ward's capacity or evidence that is sufficient to rebut the presumption by showing that the ward has or had sufficient mental capacity with respect to the matter at issue. *See Sutton v. Sutton*, 222 N.C. 274 (1942); *In re Maynard*, 64 N.C. App. 211 (1983); *Geitner v. Townsend*, 67 N.C. App. 159 (1984).

B. General Legal Status and Rights of Wards Under Plenary Guardianship

Unless otherwise provided by the Clerk's order, an order appointing a guardian for an incapacitated ward generally deprives the ward of his or her right to make his or her own decisions regarding many, if not most, issues related to his or her person, family, and property.

Even when the Clerk enters a "plenary guardianship" order, a ward should be allowed to participate, to the maximum extent of his or her capabilities, in all decisions that will affect him or her. G.S. 35A-1201(a)(5).

An incapacitated ward has the right, without the consent of his or her guardian, to file a motion seeking restoration of his or her capacity pursuant to G.S. 35A-1130.

C. Specific Legal Rights That Are or May Be Retained by Incapacitated Wards

Right to vote. An incapacitated ward has the right to register to vote and to vote in elections if he or she is otherwise qualified. 41 N.C. Atty. Gen. Op. 85 (1973).

Competency to testify as witness. An incapacitated ward is competent to testify as a witness in a civil or criminal proceeding if he or she understands the nature of one's oath to tell the truth, had sufficient capacity to observe or understand the matters about which he or she will testify, and has sufficient capacity to remember and relate those facts. *See State v. Benton*, 276 N.C. 641 (1970).

Capacity to marry, execute a will, or enter into a contract. An incapacitated ward *may* have the legal capacity to marry, to execute a will, or to enter into a contract. In each instance, the issue is whether, despite the fact that the ward has been determined to lack capacity to manage his or her own affairs or to make important decisions regarding his or her person, family, or property, the ward has the *specific* mental capacity to marry, to execute a will, or to enter into a contract. *See Medical College of Virginia v. Maynard*, 236 N.C. 506 (1953); *In re Maynard*, 64 N.C. App. 211 (1983); *Geitner v. Townsend*, 67 N.C. App. 159 (1984).

D. Specific Legal Rights That Are or Probably Are Lost by Incapacitated Wards

Driving privilege. A person who has been adjudicated incompetent under G.S. Ch. 35A is presumptively disqualified from obtaining a North Carolina driver's license. *See* G.S. 20-9(d).

Qualification as juror. A person who has been adjudicated incompetent under G.S. Ch. 35A probably is not qualified to serve on a jury in state court. *See* G.S. 9-3.

Qualification as guardian. A person who has been adjudicated incompetent under G.S. Ch. 35A is not qualified to serve as a general guardian, guardian of the person, or guardian of the estate of a minor or incapacitated person. *See* G.S. 35A-1290(c)(1).

E. Legal Rights of Wards Under Limited Guardianship

A Clerk may enter a "limited guardianship" order that expressly allows the ward to retain certain legal rights and privileges. G.S. 35A-1215(b).

F. Statutory Powers of Guardians and Limitations on the Powers of Guardians

Unless expressly limited by the Clerk's order, a guardian of the person of an incapacitated ward has all of the powers specified in G.S. 35A-1241 as well as those specified under other applicable statutes. Unless expressly limited by the Clerk's order, a guardian of the estate of an incapacitated ward has all of the powers specified in G.S. 35A-1251 as well as those specified under other applicable statutes.

A guardian's powers are subject to the limitations contained in G.S. 35A-1241, G.S. 35A-1251, other applicable statutes, and the Clerk's order. Some actions by guardians require prior court approval.

Legal proceedings involving the ward. A guardian of the person of an incapacitated ward generally does not have any authority to commence or defend on behalf of the ward a legal proceeding involving the ward or the ward's property unless the guardian is appointed as the ward's *guardian ad litem* pursuant to Rule 17 of the North Carolina Rules of Civil Procedure.

Divorce. A guardian does *not* have the authority to file an action for divorce on behalf of an incapacitated ward. *See Freeman v. Freeman,* 34 N.C. App. 301 (1977). A general guardian or guardian of the estate, however, may defend an incapacitated ward in a divorce proceeding instituted by the ward's spouse.

Sterilization. A general guardian or guardian of the person may *not* consent to the sterilization of an incapacitated ward unless the guardian obtains an order from the Clerk pursuant to G.S. 35A-1245.

Durable power of attorney. A guardian may revoke or amend a durable power of attorney executed by the ward. G.S. 32A-10.

Health care power of attorney. A general guardian or guardian of the person may not revoke a health care power of attorney executed by the ward. G.S. 32A-22. A general guardian or guardian of the person, however, may petition the court to revoke a health care power of attorney that was executed by the ward.

Advance declaration for natural death ("living will"). A general guardian or guardian of the person may not revoke a declaration of desire for natural death ("living will") executed by the ward. G.S. 35A-1208(b). In the absence of a declaration of desire for natural death executed by the ward, an incapacitated ward's guardian may authorize the withholding or withdrawal of life-prolonging measures under the circumstances specified in G.S. Ch. 90, Art. 23.

Gifts. A guardian's authority to make a gift from the ward's estate is limited. Certain types of gifts are authorized with the approval of a superior court judge. *See* G.S. Ch. 35A, Arts. 17, 18, 19.

1.8
Relationship of G.S. Ch. 35A to Other Laws

A. Incapacity Determinations in Other Civil and Criminal Proceedings

Although Article 1 of G.S. Ch. 35A establishes the exclusive procedure for adjudicating a person to be an "incompetent adult" or an "incompetent child," the issue of a person's mental "capacity" also may be determined in the context of any legal proceeding in which a person's mental capacity or incapacity is relevant and material. *See Hagins v. Greensboro Redevelopment Comm'n*, 275 N.C. 90 (1969); *In re Maynard*, 64 N.C. App. 211 (1983); *Geitner v. Townsend*, 67 N.C. App. 159 (1984); *Leonard v. England*, 115 N.C. App. 103 (1994); *Dunkley v. Shoemate*, 121 N.C. App. 360 (1996); *Soderlund v. Kuch*, 143 N.C. App. 361 (2001); *State Farm Fire & Casualty Co. v. Darsie*, 161 N.C. App. 542 (2003).

Practice Note: It is not clear whether a determination regarding a respondent's mental capacity made in the context of a civil or criminal proceeding not involving the appointment of a guardian may be asserted as collateral estoppel against the respondent in an adult guardianship proceeding under G.S. Chapter 35A.

B. Appointment of *Guardian ad Litem* under Rule 17

G.S. Ch. 35A does not limit the authority of a court to appoint a *guardian ad litem* pursuant to Rule 17 of the North Carolina Rules of Civil Procedure for an "incompetent" person who is a party to a civil action. G.S. 35A-1102 (superseding *Culton v. Culton*, 96 N.C. App. 620 (1989), *rev'd on other grounds* 327 N.C. 624 (1990); *Hagins v. Greensboro Redevelopment Comm'n*, 275 N.C. 90 (1969)). In doing so, however, a court must provide an allegedly incompetent party with notice and an opportunity to be heard and make findings, based on sufficient evidence, that the party is, in fact, "incompetent." *Hagins v. Greensboro Redevelopment Comm'n*, 275 N.C. 90 (1969).

Practice Note: Attorneys who are appointed as *guardians ad litem* pursuant to Rule 17 of the North Carolina Rules of Civil Procedure in a civil action other than a guardianship proceeding are not paid by the N.C. Office of Indigent Defense Services.

C. Adult Protective Services

North Carolina's adult protective services statute (G.S. Ch. 108A, Art. 6) authorizes the district court to order the provision of protective services to a disabled adult who needs protective services but lacks the capacity to consent to those services. *See* G.S. 108A-105. A determination that a disabled adult lacks the capacity to consent to protective services, however, does not affect proceedings to appoint a guardian for that person under G.S. Ch. 35A, and an adjudication that a person is incompetent under G.S. Ch. 35A does not affect proceedings under G.S. Ch. 108A, Art. 6. G.S. 108A-105(d).

D. Involuntary Civil Commitment

The standards and procedures for determining incapacity and appointing a guardian for an incapacitated ward are different from the procedures under G.S. Ch. 122C for the involuntary civil commitment of persons who are mentally ill or substance abusers and present a danger to themselves or others.

E. Capacity and Insanity in Criminal Proceedings

The standards and procedures for determining whether a criminal defendant lacks the capacity to stand trial or is not guilty of a crime due to insanity are different from the standard for determining whether a person is an "incompetent adult" under G.S. Ch. 35A.

F. Veterans' Guardianship Act

The provisions of the Veterans' Guardianship Act (G.S. Chapter 34), rather than those of G.S. Chapter 35A, apply with respect to the appointment of a guardian for an incompetent adult when the adult is entitled to the payment of benefits from the U.S. Department of Veterans' Affairs (VA) and federal law or regulations require the appointment of a guardian for that adult before the payment of VA benefits.

Practice Note: Clerks generally limit the authority of a guardian appointed under G.S. Chapter 34 to management of the ward's VA benefits.

G. Durable Power of Attorney

The appointment of a guardian for an incapacitated ward following the ward's execution of a durable power of attorney does not automatically revoke the durable power of attorney or limit the attorney-in-fact's authority thereunder unless the guardian revokes or amends the durable power of attorney. G.S. 32A-10(a).

H. Health Care Power of Attorney

The appointment of a guardian for an incapacitated ward following the ward's execution of a health care power of attorney does not automatically revoke the health care power of attorney or limit the health care agent's authority thereunder unless the guardian petitions a court to suspend the health care agent's authority and the court enters an order suspending the health care agent's authority. G.S. 32A-22(a).

I. Informed Consent for Medical Treatment

G.S. 90-21.13 generally authorizes a guardian, health care agent, or other authorized person to consent to medical treatment or make health care decisions on behalf of an adult who is comatose or otherwise lacks the capacity to consent to medical treatment.

J. Appointment of Representative Payee

The Social Security Act and other federal or state laws and regulations authorize the appointment of a "representative payee" to manage the federal or state public benefits or assistance payable to a person who lacks the capacity to properly manage his or her benefits or assistance. *See* 42 U.S.C. §405(j) (Social Security payments).

Appendix 1-1
Additional Resources

Outlines of the law governing incompetency and guardianship proceedings under G.S. Ch. 35A are included in volume 2 (chapters 85 and 86) of the *North Carolina Clerk of Court Procedures Manual* (Chapel Hill: School of Government, The University of North Carolina at Chapel Hill, 2003).

A pamphlet on the "Responsibilities of Guardians in North Carolina" has been published by the North Carolina Administrative Office of the Courts and is available on-line at www. nccourts.org/forms/Documents/845.pdf.

In 2004, the Governor's Advocacy Council for Persons with Disabilities produced two videotapes: "The Guardianship Process," and "Becoming a Guardian." These videotapes may be available in the offices of the Clerk of Superior Court.

CHAPTER 2:
Appointment of Attorney as *Guardian ad Litem*

2.1
Right to Counsel

A. Right to Retained or Appointed Counsel

An allegedly incapacitated respondent has the right to be represented by counsel in guardianship proceedings under G.S. Ch. 35A. G.S. 35A-1107(a). *See also Simon v. Craft*, 182 U.S. 427 (1901); *In re Deere*, 708 P.2d 1123, 1126 (Okla. 1985).

B. Right to Retain Counsel

An allegedly incapacitated respondent has the right to retain counsel of his or her own choosing if he or she has the mental capacity (and financial ability) to do so. G.S. 35A-1107(a). *See also* 98 Formal Ethics Opinion 16 (N.C. State Bar 1999).

A third party (including a relative or friend of a respondent) may retain a lawyer to represent an allegedly incapacitated respondent in an adult guardianship proceeding and pay the retained attorney's fee on behalf of the respondent as long as the respondent consents to being represented by the retained attorney and has sufficient mental capacity to consent to being represented by the retained attorney. *See* 98 Formal Ethics Opinion 16 (N.C. State Bar 1999). An attorney who has been retained by a third party to represent an allegedly incapacitated respondent in an adult guardianship proceeding may do so and accept payment of his or her attorney's fee from the third party as long as the respondent consents to being represented by the retained attorney and has sufficient mental capacity to consent to being represented by the retained attorney and the acceptance of payment from the third party will not interfere with the lawyer's professional judgment or the attorney-client relationship with the respondent or result in the disclosure of confidential client information. *See* 98 Formal Ethics Opinion 16 (N.C. State Bar 1999).

The mere fact that an attorney retained to represent an allegedly incapacitated respondent in an adult guardianship proceeding has represented the spouse or another relative of the respondent (other than a spouse or relative who is the petitioner in the pending guardianship proceeding) does not, in and of itself, constitute a conflict of interest that disqualifies the attorney from representing the respondent in the pending guardianship proceeding. *See 98 Formal Ethics Opinion 16* (N.C. State Bar 1999).

Practice Note: An attorney who is retained by or on behalf of an allegedly incapacitated respondent in an adult guardianship proceeding must comply with Rule 1.14 of the N.C. State Bar's Revised Rules of Professional Conduct if the attorney determines that the respondent's mental capacity is diminished. Rule 1.14 is discussed in more detail in § 2.6 of this chapter.

C. Constitutional and Statutory Right to Appointed Counsel

It is not clear that an allegedly incapacitated respondent has a *constitutional* right to appointed counsel in a guardianship proceeding. *See Rud v. Dahl*, 578 F.2d 674, 679 (7th Cir. 1978). *Cf. In re Gilbuena*, 209 Cal. Rptr. 556, 559–60 (Cal. Ct. App. 1985); *In re Deere*, 708 P.2d 1123, 1126 (Okla. 1985); *In re Fey*, 624 So.2d 770, 771 (Fla. Dist. Ct. App. 1993); *In re Lee*, 754 A.2d 426, 439 (Md. Ct. Spec. App. 2000).

Instead, most states provide, by statute, for the appointment of an attorney to represent an allegedly incapacitated respondent in a guardianship proceeding if the respondent is unable to retain counsel, if the respondent is indigent, or in other circumstances.

D. Appointment of Attorney as *Guardian ad Litem*

North Carolina's current guardianship statute provides for the appointment of an attorney to represent an allegedly incapacitated respondent as the respondent's *guardian ad litem* in a proceeding to appoint a guardian for the respondent pursuant to Articles 1 and 5 of G.S. Chapter 35A unless the respondent retains counsel. G.S. 35A-1107(a).

The appointment of an attorney to serve as the respondent's *guardian ad litem* pursuant to G.S. 35A-1107(a) is not dependent on a determination that the respondent is indigent. *Cf.* G.S. 7A-451(a)(13) (providing that an *indigent* person is entitled to the services of appointed counsel in adult guardianship proceedings under Article 1 of G.S. Chapter 35A).

The appointment of an attorney to serve as an allegedly incapacitated respondent's *guardian ad litem* pursuant to G.S. 35A-1107(a) does not require the court to find reasonable cause to believe that the respondent is, in fact, incapacitated. *Cf. Hagins v. Greensboro Redevelopment Comm'n*, 275 N.C. 90 (1969) (holding that a court may not appoint a *guardian ad litem* for an allegedly incapacitated party to a civil action or proceeding absent adequate notice to the party, opportunity to be heard, and sufficient evidence regarding the party's incapacity).

2.2
Appointment and Discharge of Attorney as *Guardian ad Litem*

A. Statutory Authority

G.S. 35A-1107(a) provides that when a petition is filed seeking the appointment of a guardian for an allegedly incapacitated adult, an attorney must be appointed to represent the respondent as the respondent's *guardian ad litem* unless the respondent has retained counsel.

The Clerk is not required to find that the respondent is indigent before appointing an attorney to serve as the respondent's *guardian ad litem* pursuant to G.S. 35A-1107(a). *Cf.* G.S. 7A-451(a)(13); G.S. 7A-450.

B. Appointment by Court

The Clerk of Superior Court generally is responsible for appointing an attorney to represent an allegedly incapacitated respondent in a guardianship proceeding pursuant to G.S. 35A-1107(a). The Clerk's appointment of an attorney as the respondent's *guardian ad litem*, however, must be in accordance with rules adopted by North Carolina's Office of Indigent Defense Services (IDS). G.S. 35A-1107(a); G.S. 7A-489.3(a)(3). *See also N.C. Attorney General Advisory Opinion to Malcolm Ray Hunter* (March 11, 2004).

C. Indigent Defense Services' Rules Governing Appointment

Rule 1.5 of the rules adopted by North Carolina's Office of Indigent Defense Services governs the appointment of attorneys for respondents in guardianship proceedings. In districts that have a Public Defender, the appointment generally must be made in accordance with the plan for appointment of counsel in non-criminal cases adopted by the Public Defender and approved by the Office of Indigent Defense Services. In districts that do not have a Public Defender, the appointment generally must be made on a systematic and impartial basis in accordance with the plan for appointment of counsel in non-criminal cases adopted by the judicial district bar or the county bar association, or, in the absence of such a plan, by the court. Rule 1.5 also provides that, in any district, the Office of Indigent Defense Services may provide for the appointment of counsel for respondents in guardianship proceeding in accordance with a contract, plan, or program approved by IDS. *See N.C. Attorney General Advisory Opinion to Malcolm Ray Hunter* (March 11, 2004).

An attorney may not be appointed to represent a respondent in a guardianship proceeding unless the attorney has agreed to the placement of his or her name on the list of attorneys subject to appointment in guardianship proceedings, or, if the attorney has not agreed to do so, has otherwise consented to be appointed.

IDS rules do not currently impose any special qualifications for attorneys who are appointed to represent respondents in guardianship proceedings. Special qualifications, however, may be required under local appointment plans.

An attorney who is appointed to represent a respondent in a guardianship proceeding may not delegate to another attorney any material responsibilities to the respondent unless the court finds that the substitute attorney practices in the same law firm as the appointed attorney, that the substitute attorney is on the list of attorneys who are eligible for appointment, that the substitute attorney and the respondent consent to the delegation, and that the delegation is in the respondent's best interest. IDS Rule 1.5(d)(2).

D. Discharge of Appointed Attorney

G.S. 35A-1107(a) does not expressly address the right of an allegedly incapacitated respondent to waive his or her right to be represented by appointed counsel or to discharge an attorney who has been appointed to serve as his or her *guardian ad litem*.

G.S. 35A-1107(a), however, does provide that an attorney who has been appointed to represent an allegedly incapacitated respondent as the respondent's guardian ad litem may be discharged, in accordance with any rules adopted by the Office of Indigent Defense Services, if the respondent retains counsel.

Practice Note: The IDS rules do not expressly address the circumstances under which an appointed attorney may or must be discharged in adult guardianship proceedings in which counsel has been retained by or on behalf of an allegedly incapacitated respondent. Many, if not most, Clerks are reluctant to discharge the attorney who has been appointed under G.S. 35A-1107 when counsel has been retained by or on behalf of an allegedly incapacitated respondent—often because they fear that the retained attorney represents the interests of the petitioner or a relative of the respondent, rather than the respondent's interests or because they do not believe that the respondent has sufficient mental capacity to retain counsel. If, however, an allegedly incapacitated respondent is represented by retained counsel *and* by an attorney who is appointed under G.S. 35A-1107, the role and responsibilities of the appointed attorney are even less clear than in cases in which a respondent is not represented by retained counsel and the relationship between the respondent's appointed attorney and retained counsel may be legally and professionally complex and problematic.

E. Withdrawal of Appointed Attorney

IDS Rule 1.7 governs the withdrawal of counsel appointed to represent respondents in guardianship proceedings. Under that rule, the court may, upon application of the attorney appointed to the case and for good cause shown, permit the attorney to withdraw from the case.

F. Scope of Representation by Appointed Attorney

Unless he or she is discharged or allowed to withdraw, an attorney who is appointed to represent a respondent in a guardianship proceeding represents the respondent until the guardianship petition is dismissed or until a guardian is appointed for the respondent. G.S. 35A-1107(b). If a guardian is appointed, appointed counsel must continue to represent the respondent until the entry of appeal to the appellate division or the expiration of the time for appeal. IDS Rule 1.7(a).

If a guardianship order is appealed to the Superior Court, appointed counsel must continue to represent the respondent until the superior court enters a final order deciding the appeal and until the entry of an appeal from the Superior Court's order or the expiration of the time for appeal therefrom. IDS Rule 1.7(a). If the Superior Court remands a guardianship proceeding to the Clerk of Superior Court, appointed counsel must continue to represent the respondent in connection with the proceeding on remand.

If the case is appealed to the North Carolina Court of Appeals, the Office of Appellate Defender is appointed to represent the respondent. IDS Rule 3.2(b). That Office may assign the case to an attorney within that Office or to outside counsel on the roster of appellate attorneys maintained by that Office. IDS Rule 3.2(d).

2.3
Statutory Powers and Duties of Appointed Attorney

Practice Note: An attorney who is appointed as the *guardian ad litem* for an allegedly incapacitated respondent under G.S. 35A-1107 does *not* have any authority to act as the respondent's guardian with respect to matters involving the respondent's medical care or the respondent's property. An attorney who is appointed as the *guardian ad litem* for an allegedly incapacitated respondent under G.S. 35A-1107 does *not* have the authority to act as the respondent's "emergency" or "interim" guardian.

A. Determining and Expressing the Respondent's Wishes

G.S. 35A-1107(b) requires an attorney who is appointed to represent an allegedly incapacitated respondent to

- personally visit the respondent as soon as possible following the attorney's appointment;
- make every reasonable effort to determine the respondent's wishes with respect to the guardianship proceeding; and
- present the respondent's express wishes to the court at all relevant stages of the proceeding.

B. Considering Whether Limited Guardianship Is Appropriate

G.S. 35A-1107(b) also requires appointed counsel to consider the appropriateness of limited guardianship and, if a limited guardianship is appropriate, to make recommendations to the court regarding the rights, powers, and privileges that the respondent should be allowed to retain.

C. Powers and Duties Under N.C. R. Civ. P. 17

An attorney appointed pursuant to G.S. 35A-1107 has all of the powers and duties of a *guardian ad litem* appointed to represent an incapacitated party pursuant to N.C. R. Civ. P. Rule 17, including the authority and responsibility to

- carefully investigate all facts relevant to the pending proceeding;

- secure or subpoena witnesses to testify on behalf of the respondent; and

- do all other things that are required to protect the respondent's rights and interests in connection with the pending proceeding.

Practice Note: If the respondent is represented by retained counsel, the respondent's retained attorney, rather than the attorney appointed as the respondent's *guardian ad litem*, may have the authority, in consultation with the respondent, to make decisions regarding the respondent's representation in the proceeding. *See* 98 Formal Ethics Opinion 16 (N.C. State Bar 1999).

D. Demanding an Evaluation, Closed Hearing, Jury Trial, or Appeal

---

Practice Note: If the respondent is represented by retained counsel, the respondent's retained attorney, rather than the attorney appointed as the respondent's *guardian ad litem*, may have the authority to exercise the following rights on behalf of the respondent.

G.S. Ch. 35A expressly authorizes the attorney who represents the respondent to request, on behalf of the respondent, that

- the issue of incapacity be determined by a jury;

- the hearing in a guardianship proceeding be closed to the public.

G.S. Ch. 35A implicitly authorizes the attorney who represents the respondent to

- request, on behalf of the respondent, that the court order a multidisciplinary evaluation of the respondent;

- give notice of appeal, on behalf of the respondent, from an order finding the respondent to be incapacitated or appointing a guardian for the respondent.

E. Making Recommendations Regarding the Respondent's "Best Interests"

G.S. 35A-1107(b) provides that an attorney who is serving as the respondent's *guardian ad litem* may make recommendations concerning the respondent's best interests if the respondent's best interests differ from the respondent's express wishes regarding guardianship. This issue is discussed in more detail in § 2.4 of this chapter.

F. Waiving the Respondent's Substantive Legal Rights

Neither G.S. Ch. 35A nor N.C. R. Civ. P. Rule 17 authorizes an attorney who is serving as the *guardian ad litem* for an allegedly incapacitated respondent in a guardianship proceeding to waive, compromise, or settle the respondent's substantive legal rights or to consent to the entry of a judgment against the respondent *without* the respondent's consent.

2.4
Role of Appointed Attorney or *Guardian ad Litem*

Practice Note: The discussion in this section assumes that the respondent is not represented by retained counsel. If an allegedly incapacitated respondent is represented by retained counsel and an attorney has been appointed as the respondent's guardian ad litem under G.S. 35A-1107 and is not discharged as the respondent's guardian ad litem, the role and responsibilities of the appointed attorney may be even less clear than in cases in which a respondent is not represented by retained counsel and the relationship between the respondent's appointed attorney and retained counsel may be legally and professionally problematic.

A. Attorney or *Guardian ad Litem*?

Although most state guardianship statutes nominally provide that a court-appointed lawyer acts as either the respondent's attorney or *guardian ad litem*, the role and responsibilities of court-appointed lawyers in guardianship proceedings are not always clearly defined.

G.S. 35A-1107, for example, states that the role of an attorney appointed to represent an allegedly incapacitated respondent in a guardianship proceeding generally is that of a *guardian ad litem* appointed pursuant to N.C. R. Civ. P. Rule 17. The precise nature and scope of the role and responsibilities of an attorney who is appointed as the *guardian ad litem* for an incapacitated respondent in a guardianship proceeding, however, are not entirely clear.

B. The "Zealous Advocate" and "Best Interest" Perspectives

Discussions regarding the role of lawyers who are appointed to represent allegedly incapacitated respondents in guardianship proceedings often are couched in terms of two competing models or perspectives: the "zealous advocate" model and the "best interest" perspective.

C. The "Best Interest" Perspective

Under the "best interest" perspective, the role of a court-appointed lawyer in a guardianship proceeding should be to determine, represent, and protect the respondent's "best interest." Under this model, a court-appointed lawyer acts primarily as an investigator or officer of the court rather than the respondent's attorney or a zealous advocate for the position voiced by the respondent. "In this role, the attorney determines what is in the best interest of the person who is the subject of the guardianship [proceeding,] . . . uses his or her own judgment to decide whether the person is competent, investigates the situation, and typically files a report with the court advocating what the attorney decides is in the best interest of the client." Joan L. O'Sullivan, *Role of the Attorney for the Alleged Incapacitated Person*, 31 Stetson L. Rev. 687, 687 (2001–02).

The responsibilities of a court-appointed lawyer under the "best interest" model therefore generally include

- conducting an independent and impartial investigation of the respondent's mental capacity, needs, and situation; and

- making recommendations to the court with respect to the respondent's need for a guardian, the nature and scope of the proposed guardianship, the suitability of the proposed guardian, and the respondent's best interests even if those recommendations conflict with the respondent's expressed desire or position with respect to the guardianship proceeding.

D. The "Zealous Advocate" Model

By contrast, proponents of the "zealous advocate" model contend that the role of a court-appointed attorney in guardianship proceedings is to act as "a zealous advocate for the wishes of [his or her] client." *In re Mason*, 701 A.2d 979, 982 (N.J. Super. Ch. Div. 1997). The "zealous advocate" model, therefore, requires a court-appointed lawyer to represent the allegedly incompetent respondent in a guardianship proceeding in the same manner, insofar as it is possible to do so, she would represent any client in a pending legal proceeding.

More specifically, the "zealous advocate" model requires a respondent's court-appointed lawyer to "advise the [respondent] of all the options as well as the practical and legal consequences of those options and the probability of success in pursuing any one of those options; give that advice in the language, mode of communication and terms that the [respondent] is most likely to understand; and (c) zealously advocate the course of actions chosen by the [respondent]." *Wingspan—The Second National Guardianship Conference: Recommendations*, 31 STETSON L. REV. 595, 601 (2002).

Proponents of the "zealous advocate" model contend that the potential loss of the respondent's legal rights in a guardianship proceeding requires, as a matter of public policy if not due process, that a court-appointed lawyer act as the respondent's attorney and advocate in any case in which the respondent is unable, due to indigency or incapacity, to retain legal counsel of his own choice or adequately communicate his own position regarding the guardianship proceeding to the court. They also contend that the "zealous advocate" model should apply even in cases in which the respondent's incompetency is clear or uncontested, since the respondent may need an advocate to contest other aspects of the guardianship proceeding, including the scope of the proposed guardianship, the suitability of the proposed guardian, or the residential placement or medical treatment of the respondent. *See In re M.R.*, 638 A.2d 1274, 1285 (N.J. 1994). And while proponents of the "zealous advocate" model generally recognize that a court-appointed attorney's role "does not extend to advocating [a respondent's] decisions [if they] are patently absurd or . . . pose an undue risk of harm" to the respondent, they also contend that "advocacy that is diluted by excessive concern for the [respondent's] best interests . . . raise[s] troubling questions for attorneys in an adversarial system." *In re M.R.*, 638 A.2d at 1285.

E.   "Zealous Advocate," "Best Interest," or "Both Hats?"

Courts and commentators commonly use the "zealous advocate" and "best interest" models to describe and distinguish the role of court-appointed lawyers in guardianship proceedings, often equating the "best interest" model with a lawyer's role as *guardian ad litem* and the "zealous advocate" model with a lawyer's role as the respondent's attorney. It is far from clear, however, that the "best interest" model accurately and completely describes the role of a *guardian ad litem* in guardianship proceedings *or* that the "zealous advocate" model adequately describes the role of a court-appointed lawyer who acts as the attorney for an allegedly incompetent respondent.

As noted above, the "zealous advocate" model does not require that an attorney always advocate the positions or wishes of her client. And the rules of professional conduct (N.C. Revised Rules of Professional Conduct, Rule 1.14) governing lawyers allow a lawyer to make decisions on behalf of a client if the client's mental incapacity prevents him from making appropriate decisions in connection with a legal proceeding and the lawyer's actions are in the client's "best interest." Nor is there an exact correlation between the "best interest" model and the role and responsibilities of a *guardian ad litem* for an allegedly incompetent adult.

So while the "zealous advocate" and "best interest" models may provide a general context for discussing the role of court-appointed lawyers in guardianship proceedings, their usefulness is limited and they are not determinative.

As a result of this ambiguity and confusion, some lawyers who are appointed to represent allegedly incapacitated respondents in guardianship proceedings simply choose whichever role they prefer. Some choose what they may perceive to be the "easier" or "safer" role— simply investigating the facts and presenting information to the court. Others believe that they should act in what they perceive to be the respondent's "best interest," rather than acting as a "zealous advocate" for the respondent or the respondent's expressed wishes. And others believe that they can and should act as zealous advocates, opposing the appointment of a guardian for the allegedly incompetent respondent, if the respondent desires to do so, without regard to whether guardianship is in the respondent's "best interest."

The result of choosing one role rather than the other, however, may be that "some important functions [that should be performed by an attorney or *guardian ad litem*] may never be performed by anyone [and] other functions may be performed by persons who do not have the training to perform them properly. . . ." James M. Peden, *The Guardian ad litem Under the Guardianship Reform Act: A Profusion of Duties, a Confusion of Roles*, 68 U. Det. L. Rev. 19, 29 (1990–91).

Confronted with the dilemma of whether to act as the respondent's attorney or *guardian ad litem*, some court-appointed lawyers attempt to "wear both hats." *See* A. Frank Johns, *Guardianship from 1978 to 1988 in View of Restructure* (N.C. Bar Foundation, 1988). And while this is not a problem *if* and to the extent that the responsibilities of these two roles are consistent with each other and with state law, some courts and commentators believe that the roles of attorney and *guardian ad litem* are "materially different," are potentially, if not inherently, incompatible, and should not be performed simultaneously by one person. *See*

In re Lee, 754 A.2d 426, 438 (Md. Spec. Ct. App. 2000) ("the duties of an attorney may at times conflict with the duties of a *guardian ad litem*"); Vicki Gottlich, *The Role of the Attorney for the Defendant in Adult Guardianship Cases: An Advocate's Perspective*, 7 MD. J. CONTEMP. L. ISSUES 191, 194 (1995–96); Sally Balch Hurme, *Current Trends in Guardianship Reform*, 7 MD. J. CONTEMP. L. ISSUES 143, 151 (1995–96) (suggesting that in most cases, "the same person cannot, and should not, serve in both roles simultaneously"); Elizabeth R. Calhoun and Suzanna L. Basinger, *Right to Counsel in Guardianship Proceedings*, 33 CLEARINGHOUSE REV. 316, 319 (Sept.–Oct. 1999). *See also* G.S. 7B-602(c) and G.S. 7B-1101(c) (prohibiting an attorney from acting as both the attorney and *guardian ad litem* for a parent in a juvenile court proceeding).

2.5
Professional and Ethical Responsibilities of Appointed Attorney

A. General Scope of the Rules of Professional Conduct

All North Carolina attorneys, including attorneys who are appointed as *guardians ad litem* for respondents in guardianship proceedings, are subject to the requirements and limitations contained in the North Carolina State Bar's Revised Rules of Professional Conduct (RPC). Some of the RPC, however, "create duties that are owed only in the professional client-lawyer relationship" while "other rules . . . apply . . . [even when] a lawyer is acting in a non-professional capacity." 2004 Formal Ethics Opinion 11 (North Carolina State Bar, Jan. 21, 2005).

B. Application of the Rules to Lawyers Who Are Appointed as *Guardians ad Litem*

The extent to which lawyers who are appointed as *guardians ad litem* in guardianship proceedings are subject to the RPC, therefore, depends on whether the lawyers who are appointed to represent allegedly incapacitated respondents under G.S. 35A-1107 have a client-lawyer relationship with the respondent, or whether they are acting in a "non-professional capacity" when they are serving as *guardians ad litem*.

The North Carolina State Bar's ethics committee recently addressed a similar issue in the context of lawyers who are appointed, pursuant to G.S. 7B-1101(1) and Rule 17, as guardians ad litem for "incapacitated" parents who are respondents in juvenile proceedings involving termination of parental rights. *See* 2004 Formal Ethics Opinion 11; *see also In re Shepard*, 162 N.C. App. 215 (2004). The ethics committee ruled that if another lawyer is appointed as the parent's attorney, the lawyer who is appointed as the parent's *guardian ad litem* "does not have a client-lawyer relationship with the parent, and therefore, would not be governed by the Rules of Professional Conduct relating to duties owed to clients."

Thus, a court-appointed lawyer who acts "purely as a guardian [ad litem] and not [as] an attorney" is *not* bound by the ethical rules governing confidentiality (Rule 1.6), zealous advocacy (Rule 1.3), loyalty (Rules 1.7 through 1.10), or evaluations for use by third persons (Rule 2.3), but is subject to the ethical rules governing candor toward the court

(Rule 3.3), fairness to opposing party and counsel (Rule 3.4), ex parte communications with and unlawful influence of judicial officials (Rule 3.5), and dishonesty, fraud, deceit, misrepresentation, and conduct prejudicial to the administration of justice (Rule 8.4).

The committee, however, also ruled that if a court appoints a lawyer to act as a party's attorney and *guardian ad litem*, the lawyer must comply with the Rules of Professional Conduct that apply to client-lawyer relationships. Given the ambiguity regarding the role of lawyers who are appointed to represent respondents in guardianship proceedings, a lawyer who is appointed under G.S. 35A-1107 may be acting as the respondent's attorney *and guardian ad litem* in cases in which the respondent has not retained counsel. And if this is so, a lawyer who is appointed as the *guardian ad litem* for an unrepresented respondent in a guardianship proceeding is subject to the Rules of Professional Conduct that govern client-lawyer relationships.

C. Responsibilities as a "Zealous Advocate"

When a lawyer has an attorney-client relationship with a client, the RPC generally require the lawyer to act, within the bounds of law and insofar as possible, as a "zealous advocate" for her client. The official comments to Rule 1.3 of the North Carolina State Bar's Revised Rules of Professional Conduct require a lawyer to "act with commitment and dedication to the interests of the client and with zeal in advocacy upon the client's behalf." In representing a client, a lawyer is required to "abide by a client's decisions concerning the objectives of representation and . . . consult with the client as to the means by which they are to be pursued." RPC Rule 1.2. In representing a client, however, a lawyer may exercise her professional judgment to waive or fail to assert a right or position of the client and may exercise professional discretion in determining the means by which a matter should be pursued. RPC Rule 1.2(a)(3); RPC Rule 1.4 (Comment 1). *Cf. State v. Ali*, 329 N.C. 391, 403 (1991).

A lawyer's professional obligation to act as a zealous advocate for her client "is not a license to raise frivolous defenses or to stand obdurately on procedural points." *See* O'Sullivan, 7 Md. J. Contemp. Legal Issues at 68; *see also* RPC Rule 3.1; RPC Rule 1.2(a)(2). It does, however, require a court-appointed lawyer to

- communicate with her client;

- explain the potential legal consequences of and the legal options with respect to the pending litigation to the client;

- ascertain the client's wishes with respect to pending litigation;

- secure and present evidence and arguments on behalf of the client; and

- take appropriate actions (such as objecting to inadmissible evidence and cross-examining adverse witnesses) necessary to protect the client's legal rights and interests in the litigation.

At a minimum, the rule of "zealous advocacy" requires a lawyer who is appointed as the attorney and *guardian ad litem* for an allegedly incapacitated respondent in a guardianship proceeding to ensure that

- the respondent is not found to be incompetent in the face of insufficient evidence;

- guardianship is not ordered if there are appropriate and less restrictive alternatives available to protect the respondent's interests;

- the guardian appointed for an incompetent respondent is suitable and qualified; and

- appropriate limits are placed on the guardianship when necessary to protect the respondent's rights and interests.

D. Responsibility to Protect Client Confidences and Secrets

If a court-appointed lawyer acts as the attorney and *guardian ad litem* for a respondent in a guardianship proceeding, the lawyer has an ethical and professional obligation to protect the respondent's confidences and secrets and is prohibited from revealing information about the respondent acquired during the attorney-client relationship unless the respondent gives informed consent to the disclosure or disclosure is authorized under the Revised Rules of Professional Conduct. *See* 2004 Formal Ethics Opinion 11.

E. Other Professional Responsibilities When Representing Clients

In addition, a lawyer who is appointed as the respondent's attorney and *guardian ad litem* is subject to the State Bar's rules governing

- communication with a client (Rule 1.4);

- competent legal representation (Rule 1.1);

- loyalty to a client and conflicts of interest (Rules 1.7 through 1.10);

- terminating legal representation (Rule 1.16);

- undertaking evaluations for use by third parties (Rule 2.3);

- the assertion of nonmeritorious claims or defenses (Rule 3.1);

- dilatory practices and delaying litigation (Rule 3.2);

- candor toward the court (Rule 3.3);

- fairness to the opposing party and counsel (Rule 3.4);

- *ex parte* communications with judicial officials and unlawful attempts to influence judicial officials (Rule 3.5);

- testifying as a witness at trial (Rule 3.7);

- making false statements of law or fact to others (Rule 4.1);

- communication with persons represented by counsel (Rule 4.2);

- dealing with unrepresented persons (Rule 4.3);

- respect for the rights of others (Rule 4.4);

- dishonesty, fraud, deceit, misrepresentation, and conduct prejudicial to the administration of justice (Rule 8.4); and

- representing clients with diminished mental capacity (Rule 1.14).

2.6
Representing Persons with Diminished Capacity

A. RPC Rule 1.14

If a lawyer who is appointed as the *guardian ad litem* for a respondent in a guardianship proceeding is subject to the ethical and professional rules governing client-lawyer relationships, the lawyer's representation of the allegedly incompetent respondent may be affected by RPC Rule 1.14, which governs a lawyer's representation of a client with diminished mental capacity. The rule states:

(a) When a client's capacity to make adequately considered decisions in connection with a representation is diminished, whether because of minority, mental impairment or for some other reason, the lawyer shall, as far as reasonably possible, maintain a normal client-lawyer relationship with the client.

(b) When the lawyer reasonably believes that the client has diminished capacity, is at risk of substantial physical, financial or other harm unless action is taken and cannot adequately act in the client's own interest, the lawyer may take reasonably necessary protective action including consulting with individuals or entities that have the ability to take action to protect the client and, in appropriate cases, seeking the appointment of a *guardian ad litem* or guardian.

(c) Information relating to the representation of a client with diminished capacity is protected by Rule 1.6. When taking protective action pursuant to paragraph (b), the lawyer is impliedly authorized under Rule 1.6(a) to reveal information about the client, but only to the extent reasonably necessary to protect the client's interests.

Because an adult respondent in guardianship proceedings is alleged to be mentally incapacitated or incompetent, a court-appointed lawyer who acts as the attorney and *guardian ad litem* for an allegedly incompetent respondent must consider whether and to what extent Rule 1.14 applies with respect to her representation of the respondent.

B. Role and Responsibilities of Lawyers Under Rule 1.14

"Representing a questionably competent client is always an enormous challenge. . . . The client may be confused about some things, but not about others. He or she may make bad decisions and insist that the lawyer advocate for him or her, or may demand that the lawyer defend a seemingly indefensible position." Joan L. O'Sullivan, *Role of the Attorney for the Alleged Incapacitated Person*, 31 Stetson L. Rev. 687, 725 (2001–02).

If a court-appointed lawyer representing an allegedly incapacitated respondent in a guardianship proceeding determines that the respondent's capacity to make adequately considered decisions in connection with the pending proceeding is diminished due to a mental impairment, the lawyer must, as far as reasonably possible, maintain a normal attorney-client relationship with the respondent.

Comment 1 to Rule 1.14 reminds lawyers that "a client with diminished capacity often has the ability to understand, deliberate upon, and reach conclusions about matters affecting the client's own well-being." Thus, the North Carolina State Bar's ethics committee has ruled that an attorney may represent an allegedly incompetent respondent in opposing adjudication of the respondent's incompetency and appointment of a guardian if (a) the respondent instructs the attorney to do so, (b) the attorney determines that the respondent has sufficient mental capacity to make an adequately considered decision to oppose the guardianship petition, and (c) opposing the petition does not require the attorney to present a frivolous claim or defense on behalf of the respondent or violate another rule of professional conduct. *See* 1998 Formal Ethics Opinion 16.

Protective action by lawyer. Rule 1.14, however, allows a lawyer to take "protective action" on behalf of a client (and presumably contrary to the client's expressed wishes) if the lawyer determines that the client's mental impairment is such that he cannot make adequately considered decisions that will adequately protect his interests in connection with a legal proceeding and is thereby at risk of substantial physical, financial, or other harm. (Even in these instances, however, the lawyer may disclose confidential information about the client only to the extent reasonably necessary to protect the client's interests.) Similarly, comments 9 and 10 to Rule 1.14 allow a lawyer to take legal action on behalf of a person whose mental capacity is so severely diminished that he cannot establish a client-lawyer relationship with the attorney or make or express considered judgments about a legal matter *if* a person acting in good faith on behalf of the incapacitated person requests the lawyer to act on behalf of the incapacitated person and legal action is required to avoid imminent and irreparable harm to the health, safety, or financial interests of the incapacitated individual. And comment 7 to Rule 1.14 suggests that any protective action that a lawyer takes on behalf of a client with diminished capacity should be "guided by such factors as the wishes and values of the client to the extent known, the client's best interests and the goals of intruding into the client's decision-making autonomy to the least extent feasible, maximizing client capacities and respecting the client's family and social connections."

Lawyer's authority to make decisions for client. Similarly, the Restatement (Third) of the Law Governing Lawyers states that when a lawyer determines that a client is unable to make adequately considered decisions regarding the matter of legal representation, the lawyer may pursue her reasonable view of the client's objectives or interests as the client would define them if able to make adequately considered decisions—even if the client expresses no wishes or gives contrary instructions.

When a client's disability prevents maintaining a normal client-lawyer relationship and there is no guardian or other legal representative to make decisions for the client, the lawyer may be justified in making decisions with respect to questions within the scope of the representation that would normally be made by the client. A lawyer should act only on a reasonable belief, based on appropriate investigation, that the client is unable to make an adequately considered decision rather than simply being confused or misguided. *See* RESTATEMENT (THIRD) OF THE LAW GOVERNING LAWYERS § 24, Comment d.

***"Zealous advocacy" and "best interest" under Rule 1.**14. In some instances, ethical and professional rules may require a court-appointed lawyer to oppose adjudication of the respondent's incompetency, to oppose the appointment of a guardian or interim guardian, to oppose the appointment of a particular person as guardian or interim guardian, or to propose a limited, rather than plenary, guardianship. In other instances, though, the rules may justify the lawyer's conceding the respondent's incompetency or accepting the appointment of a guardian to manage the respondent's affairs. In the case of a comatose (or a severely delusional, demented, or cognitively impaired) respondent, Rule 1.14 clearly allows a court-appointed lawyer to take legal action on behalf of the respondent in a guardianship proceeding to the extent necessary to protect the respondent's health, safety, or financial interests from imminent and irreparable harm. Thus, a court-appointed lawyer may act, with little or no guidance from a severely incapacitated respondent, to ensure that "(1) there is no less restrictive alternative to guardianship; (2) proper due-process procedure is followed; (3) the petitioner proves the allegations in the petition [as required by law] . . .; (4) the proposed guardian is a suitable person to serve; and (5) if a guardian is appointed, the order leaves the client with as much autonomy as possible." O'Sullivan, 31 STETSON L. REV. at 726.

On the other hand, though, a court-appointed lawyer who acts as the attorney and *guardian ad litem* for an allegedly incompetent adult in a guardianship proceeding may *not* disclose confidential information to the court without the respondent's consent and may *not* make recommendations to the court regarding the respondent's best interests *if* those interests differ from the respondent's express wishes *and* the respondent's mental impairment does not prevent his making adequately considered decisions that will adequately protect her interests in connection with the guardianship proceeding. *In re Lee*, 754 A.2d 426, 439–41 (Md. Ct. Spec. App. 2000).

C. Assessing a Client's Mental Capacity

In assessing a respondent's mental capacity, lawyers should remember that a person does not lack capacity merely because a guardianship proceeding has been brought against him or he "does things that other people find disagreeable or difficult to understand. Indeed, a great danger in capacity assessment is that eccentricities, aberrant character traits, or risk-taking decisions will be confused with incapacity. A capacity assessment first asks what kind of person is being assessed and what sorts of things that person has generally held to be important." Charles P. Sabatino, *Representing a Client with Diminished Capacity: How Do You Know It And What Do You Do About It?* 16 J. AM. ACAD. OF MATRIMONIAL LAWYERS 481, 486 (2000).

And because capacity may be "affected by countless variables: time, place, social setting, emotional, mental or physical states, etc.," capacity assessment should be approached in "two stages—first take reasonable steps to optimize capacity; and second, perform a preliminary assessment of capacity." Sabatino, 16 J. AM. ACAD. OF MATRIMONIAL LAWYERS at 486–99.

Assessment of a respondent's cognitive capacity should focus on the respondent's decision-making *process* more than the decisional *output* of the respondent's reasoning. The issue is whether the respondent's reasoning process is significantly impaired, not whether the respondent's decisions are, in an objective sense, reasonable. In assessing a respondent's cognitive capacity, the issue is not whether the respondent's cognitive abilities are impaired, subaverage, or suboptimal, but rather whether the respondent's cognitive abilities are at least minimally sufficient to make important decisions.

A court-appointed lawyer, therefore, should consider several factors in assessing a respondent's cognitive capacity:

- awareness (extent of the respondent's capacity to perceive, concentrate, remember information);
- comprehension (ability to understand and assimilate information);
- reasoning (ability to integrate and rationally evaluate information);
- deliberation (ability to weigh facts and alternatives in light of personal values and potential consequences);
- understanding (ability to appreciate the nature of the situation and the possible consequences of one's decisions);
- choice (ability to express in a sufficiently stable and consistent manner one's preference or decision).

Similarly, comment 6 to Rule 1.14 states:

> In determining the extent of the client's diminished capacity, the lawyer should consider and balance such factors as: the client's ability to articulate reasoning leading to a decision, variability of state of mind and ability to appreciate consequences of a decision; the substantive fairness of a decision; and the consistency of a decision with known long-term commitments and values of the client.

Standard screening tests, such as the Mini-Mental Status Examination (MMSE) or the Short Portable Status Questionnaire (SPSQ), may be useful in making preliminary assessments of a respondent's mental capacity. These tests, however, "provide only a crude global assessment of cognitive functioning" and do not establish or "rule out the ability to perform some decisionmaking tasks." Sabatino, 16 J. Am. Acad. of Matrimonial Lawyers at 493. Thus, in appropriate circumstances a lawyer may, and should, seek guidance from an appropriate diagnostician regarding the nature and extent of a respondent's incapacity. RPC Rule 1.14, Comment 6.

D. Communicating with Persons with Diminished Capacity: Practice Pointers

In a case involving a person with diminished mental capacity, the lawyer's communication with the person must take into account the person's mental capacity. For example, persons who suffer from Alzheimer's disease may experience "sundowner syndrome," becoming more confused around dusk. A lawyer representing a person with Alzheimer's disease, therefore, should communicate with the person early in the morning or after a meal. Similarly, lawyers should use simple terms and concrete examples in explaining legal proceedings and the possible consequences of guardianship to persons with diminished mental capacity. *See* O'Sullivan, 31 Stetson L. Rev. at 715, 727–28.

A person's physical condition, such as hearing loss, also should be taken into consideration in determining the attorney's obligations under Rule 1.4. Lawyers can attempt to enhance their communication with elderly or impaired clients by printing documents in large type, speaking in plain language and avoiding legalese, sending materials to clients for review before meetings, and minimizing background noise and distractions. Jan Ellen Rein, *Ethics and the Questionably Competent Client: What the Model Rules Say and Don't Say*, 9 Stan. L. & Policy Rev. 241, 244 (1998). Another useful technique to test the client's understanding of advice or explanations provided by a lawyer is to ask the client to paraphrase (not merely repeat) what the lawyer said.

2.7
Compensation of Appointed and Retained Attorneys for Respondents

If a respondent is not determined to be incapacitated and the court finds that the petitioner did not have reasonable grounds to bring the proceeding, the reasonable fee for respondent's appointed counsel as determined by the court must be taxed to and paid by the petitioner. G.S. 35A-1116(c)(2).

If a respondent is determined to be incapacitated and the respondent is not indigent, the reasonable fee for respondent's appointed counsel as determined by the court must be taxed to and paid by the respondent or the respondent's estate. G.S. 35A-1116(c)(1).

If an indigent respondent is determined to be incapacitated, the reasonable fee for respondent's appointed counsel, as determined by the court in accordance with IDS rules, must be submitted to and paid by the Office of Indigent Defense Services in accordance with IDS rules. G.S. 35A-1116(c)(3); IDS Rule 1.9.

2.8
Civil Liability of Appointed Attorneys

The North Carolina Supreme Court has held that a person who is appointed to serve as a *guardian ad litem* for an incapacitated party to a civil action may be held liable for damages resulting from his or her failure to exercise due diligence in the protection of the party's rights and estate. *Travis v. Johnston*, 244 N.C. 713, 722 (1956).

A recent decision by the North Carolina Court of Appeals, however, suggests that attorneys who are appointed to represent allegedly incapacitated respondents in guardianship proceedings are entitled to quasi-judicial immunity from civil liability in connection with the exercise of their official duties in guardianship proceedings. *Dalenko v. Wake County Dept. of Human Services*, 157 N.C. App. 49, 56–58 (2003). *Cf. Collins v. Tabet*, 806 P.2d 40, 48 (N.M. 1991).

Appendix 2-1
Additional Resources

The role and responsibilities of appointed counsel in guardianship proceedings are discussed in more detail in John L. Saxon, *The Role and Responsibilities of Court-Appointed Lawyers in Guardianship Proceedings*, ADMINISTRATION OF JUSTICE BULLETIN No. 2005/06 (Chapel Hill: School of Government, The University of North Carolina at Chapel Hill, 2005), available online at www.sog.unc.edu/pubs/electronicversions/pdfs/aojb0506.pdf.

RPC Rule 1.14 is discussed in detail in Jan Ellen Rein, *Ethics and the Questionably Competent Client: What the Model Rules Say and Don't Say*, 9 STAN. L. & POLICY REV. 241 (1998), and in Elizabeth Laffitte, *Model Rule 1.14: The Well-Intended Rule Still Leaves Some Questions Unanswered*, 17 GEORGETOWN J. LEGAL ETHICS 313 (2003). *See also* RESTATEMENT (THIRD) OF THE LAW GOVERNING LAWYERS § 24.

Some of the professional and ethical obligations of lawyers who act as the attorneys for allegedly incompetent respondents in guardianship proceedings are discussed in greater detail in Joan L. O'Sullivan, *Role of the Attorney for the Alleged Incapacitated Person*, 31 STETSON L. REV. 687, 713–19 (2001–02), and in Vicki Gottlich, *The Role of the Attorney for the Defendant in Adult Guardianship Cases: An Advocate's Perspective*, 7 MD. J. CONTEMP. L. ISSUES 191, 201–07 (1995–96).

Issues regarding the legal representation of older adults and persons with diminished capacity also are addressed in: *Assessment of Older Adults with Diminished Capacity: A Handbook for Lawyers* (Washington, DC: ABA Commission on Law and Aging, 2005); *Representing Older Persons with Diminished Capacity: Ethical Considerations* (Washington, DC: AARP National Legal Training Project, 2005); Charles P. Sabatino, *Representing a Client with Diminished Capacity: How Do You Know It And What Do You Do About It?* 16 J. AM. ACAD. OF MATRIMONIAL LAWYERS 481, 486 (2000); and Erica Wood and Audrey K. Straight, *Effective Counseling of Older Clients: The Attorney-Client Relationship* (Washington, DC: ABA Commission on Legal Problems of the Elderly, 1995).

CHAPTER 3:
Jurisdiction and Venue

3.1
Subject Matter Jurisdiction

A. The Clerk of Superior Court's Jurisdiction

Original jurisdiction. The Clerk of Superior Court has original jurisdiction, and in most cases original and exclusive jurisdiction, over legal proceedings to appoint a guardian for an incapacitated adult pursuant to G.S. Ch. 35A. G.S. 35A-1103(a); G.S. 35A-1203(a). *See also In re Simmons*, 266 N.C. 702 (1966).

The Clerk also has original jurisdiction over proceedings to restore the capacity of an incapacitated ward, to appoint an ancillary guardian, to remove guardians, to appoint successor guardians, to adjust the amount of a guardian's bond, to determine disputes between guardians, and to ensure compliance with the court's orders and statutory requirements related to guardianship of incapacitated persons. G.S. 35A-1130; G.S. 35A-1203; G.S. 35A-1207; G.S. 35A-1280. *See also Cline v. Teich*, 92 N.C. App. 257 (1988); *In re Ward*, 337 N.C. 443 (1994).

Judicial authority of Assistant Clerks of Superior Court. The Clerk's judicial authority in guardianship proceedings may be exercised by the Clerk of Superior Court or by an Assistant Clerk of Superior Court. G.S. 1-13; G.S. 7A-103(14); G.S. 7A-103(16); G.S. 7A-102(b).

Family court programs in the District Court Division. In 1998, the General Assembly enacted legislation authorizing the establishment of "Family Court" programs in the District Court Division of the General Court of Justice and provided that district court judges assigned to Family Court had jurisdiction to hear and decide all matters involving "intrafamily rights, relationships, and obligations . . . including . . . guardianship. . . ." S.L. 1998-202, §25. In practice, however, Family Courts in North Carolina have not exercised jurisdiction over proceedings under G.S. Ch. 35A to appoint guardians for allegedly incapacitated adults.

B. The Jurisdiction of Superior Court Judges

If the Clerk "has an interest, direct or indirect, in" a proceeding involving the appointment of a guardian for an allegedly incapacitated respondent, subject matter jurisdiction over the proceeding is vested in the Superior Court and may be exercised by any superior court judge residing or presiding in the district. G.S. 35A-1103(d).

G.S. 7A-104(a) lists several circumstances under which a Clerk is disqualified from exercising judicial authority with respect to an estate matter or other legal proceeding. Neither G.S. 35A-1103(d) nor G.S. 7A-104, however, specify the procedures for transferring subject matter jurisdiction from the Clerk to a Superior Court Judge.

Appellate Jurisdiction. The appellate jurisdiction of Superior Court Judges is discussed in Chapter 9 of this manual.

3.2
Personal Jurisdiction

A. Grounds for Exercising Personal Jurisdiction

G.S. Ch. 35A does not address directly the State's authority to exercise personal jurisdiction over an allegedly incapacitated person in a proceeding seeking the appointment of a guardian for that person.

G.S. 1-75.4(1), however, provides that a North Carolina court may exercise personal jurisdiction over a person who has been served pursuant to N.C. R. Civ. P. Rule 4(j) or Rule 4(j1) if the person against whom the claim is asserted is, at the time of service of process, a natural person who is

- present in the State; *or*
- domiciled in the State.

B. Domicile and Personal Jurisdiction

An adult is "domiciled" in North Carolina if she actually resides in North Carolina and has the present intention of continuing to reside in the State permanently or indefinitely or if she was domiciled in North Carolina, is absent from the State, and has not established a new domicile elsewhere. *See Sherwood v. Sherwood*, 29 N.C. App. 112 (1976).

An adult who has been adjudicated mentally incompetent, however, generally lacks the capacity to change her domicile and therefore is deemed to remain domiciled in the state in which she was domiciled prior to becoming incompetent, regardless of whether she has subsequently moved to another state. *See Lawson v. Langley*, 211 N.C. 526 (1937). The same is probably true with respect to an adult who has not been adjudicated incompetent but is, in fact, incompetent when he moves or is moved from the state of his domicile to another state.

C. Service of Process and Personal Jurisdiction

To exercise personal jurisdiction over a respondent in a guardianship proceeding, the Clerk must find that the respondent has been served with process or notice in accordance with G.S. 35A-1109.

3.3
Interstate Jurisdictional Issues

Potential interstate jurisdictional conflicts arise in guardianship proceedings when an allegedly incapacitated respondent's domicile is unclear, when the respondent is domiciled in one state but is residing or present in a different state, or when the respondent moves or is moved from one state to another and both a North Carolina Clerk of Superior Court and a court in another state assert, are asked to assert, or could assert jurisdiction over a proceeding to appoint a guardian for the respondent.

The Uniform Adult Guardianship and Protective Proceedings Jurisdiction Act. In 2007, the National Conference of Commissioners on Uniform State Laws approved a Uniform Adult Guardianship and Protective Proceedings Jurisdiction Act (UAGPPJA), which establishes rules and procedures for minimizing and resolving interstate jurisdictional conflicts in guardianship proceedings. North Carolina, however, has not enacted the UAGPPJA or other legislation regarding interstate jurisdictional conflicts in guardianship cases.

3.4
Venue

A. Definition of Venue

Venue refers to the county in which a guardianship proceeding should be filed and heard.

B. Distinction Between Venue and Jurisdiction

Venue is distinct and different from jurisdiction. The fact that a guardianship proceeding is filed and heard in a county that is not the proper venue for the proceeding does not affect the Clerk's jurisdiction over the matter or the validity of the Clerk's order appointing a guardianship for the respondent. *See Nello L. Teer Co. v. Hitchcock Corp.*, 235 N.C. 741 (1952). *Cf. Duke v. Johnston*, 211 N.C. 171 (1937) (interpreting the *venue* provisions in a prior version of North Carolina's guardianship law to render void for lack of jurisdiction the appointment of a guardian by the Clerk of a county other than the county in which the ward resided).

C. Proper Venue for Adult Guardianship Proceedings

G.S. 35A-1103(b) and G.S. 35A-1204(a) provide that the proper venue for a proceeding to appoint a guardian for an allegedly incapacitated adult under G.S. Ch. 35A is the county in which the respondent

- resides; or

- is domiciled; or

- is an inpatient in a treatment facility.

If the respondent's residence or domicile cannot be determined, the proper venue for the proceeding is the county in which the respondent is present or found. G.S. 35A-1103(b).

Venue for the appointment of an ancillary guardian pursuant to G.S. 35A-1280 is in any county in which the nonresident ward owns real property or, if the nonresident ward does not have an interest in real property in the State, in any county in which the nonresident ward owns or has an interest in personal property. G.S. 35A-1204(c).

Simultaneous proceedings in two counties. If venue is proper in two different counties and guardianship proceedings involving the same respondent are brought in both counties, venue lies in the county in which the proceedings were first commenced. G.S. 35A-1103(c).

3.5
Change of Venue

A. Waiver of Improper Venue

If a guardianship proceeding is filed in a county in which venue is not proper, the issue of improper venue is waived unless raised by a timely motion objecting to improper venue pursuant to N.C. R. Civ. P. Rule 12(b)(3).

B. Motion and Order for Change of Venue

G.S. 35A-1104 authorizes a Clerk, on motion of a party or on the Clerk's own motion, to order a change of venue in a guardianship proceeding if the Clerk finds that the change of venue will not result in any hardship or prejudice to the respondent.

C. Transfer of Venue Following Determination of Incapacity

G.S. 35A-1204 authorizes a Clerk, at any time before or after appointing a guardian for an incapacitated adult, to transfer venue of a guardianship proceeding to a different county on motion of a party or on the Clerk's own motion.

3.6
Abatement

The death of an allegedly incapacitated respondent during the pendency of a proceeding to appoint a guardian for the respondent abates the proceeding. *In re Higgins*, 160 N.C. App. 704 (2003).

Appendix 3-1
Additional Resources

Interstate jurisdictional issues in guardianship proceedings are discussed in more detail in: Vicki Gottlich, *Finders, Keepers, Losers, Weepers: Conflict of Laws in Adults Guardianship Cases*, 23 CLEARINGHOUSE REV. 1415 (1990); A. Frank Johns, *Subject-Matter Jurisdiction, Domicil(e) and the Jet-Age Independence of Vulnerable Adults*, 1 NAT'L GUARDIANSHIP J. 291 (Fall 1990); A. Frank Johns, Vicki Gottlich, and Marlis Carson, *Guardianship Jurisdiction Revisited: A Proposal for a Uniform Act*, 26 CLEARINGHOUSE REV. 647 (Oct. 1992); Sally Balch Hurme, *Mobile Guardianships: Partial Solutions to Interstate Jurisdictional Problems*, NAT'L ACAD. OF ELDER LAW ATTYS. Q. 6 (Summer 2004).

A copy of the final draft of the Uniform Adult Guardianship and Protective Proceedings Jurisdiction Act is available on-line: www.law.upenn.edu/bll/archives/ulc/ugijaea/2007am_final.pdf.

CHAPTER 4:
Parties, Pleadings, and Notice

4.1
Parties

The parties in a proceeding to appoint a guardian for an allegedly incapacitated adult are the petitioner (or petitioners), the respondent, any person other than the petitioner who files an application requesting the appointment of a guardian for the respondent, and any other person who is properly joined as a party to the proceeding.

A. Petitioner

Any individual, corporation, or other person, including a nonresident petitioner, a disinterested public agent, or any state or local human services agency acting through its authorized representative, may file a petition seeking a determination of a respondent's incapacity and the appointment of a guardian for the respondent. G.S. 35A-1104; G.S. 35A-1210.

Although guardianship proceedings often are initiated by the spouse, an adult child, a relative, or friend of the respondent, there is no requirement that the petitioner have any particular relationship to the respondent.

Although guardianship proceedings may be initiated by a county social services department or other human services agency, state law does not expressly require county social services departments or other human services agencies to initiate proceedings to appoint guardians for allegedly incapacitated adults or to provide legal, financial, or social services to allegedly incapacitated adults or their families in connection with guardianship proceedings.

Practice Note: Although G.S. Chapter 35A does not require a county social services department to initiate an adult guardianship proceeding, Article 6 of G.S. Chapter 108A does require county social services departments to respond to reports regarding the abuse, neglect, or exploitation of disabled adults and to provide protective services, including, in certain circumstances, guardianship services, to disabled adults who need protective services.

B. Applicant

Any individual, corporation, disinterested public agent, or state or local human services agency may file an application for the appointment of a guardian for an allegedly incapacitated adult. G.S. 35A-1210. An application for the appointment of a guardian for an allegedly incapacitated adult may be joined with or filed subsequently to the filing of a petition seeking a determination of the respondent's incapacity. G.S. 35A-1210. When an application for the appointment of a guardian for an allegedly incapacitated adult is filed by a person other than the petitioner who filed a petition seeking a determination of the respondent's incapacity, the applicant, as well as the petitioner, is a party to the proceeding.

C. Respondent

The allegedly incapacitated adult who is the subject of a pending guardianship proceeding is a party to the proceeding.

D. *Guardian ad litem* and Counsel for Respondent

Although G.S. 35A-1109 requires that a respondent's counsel or *guardian ad litem* be served with the petition and notice of hearing in a guardianship proceeding, and other provisions of G.S. 35A authorize the respondent's counsel or *guardian ad litem* to exercise some or all of the respondent's rights as a party on the respondent's behalf, the respondent's retained or appointed counsel or *guardian ad litem* is *not* a party to the proceeding.

E. Respondent's Next of Kin and Other Interested Persons

Although G.S. 35A-1109 requires that the respondent's next of kin and other interested persons as designated by the Clerk be given notice of a pending guardianship proceeding, those persons are not parties to the proceeding unless they or the Clerk take some additional action that results in their becoming or being joined as parties to the proceeding.

The respondent's next of kin or other interested persons may become parties to a pending guardianship proceeding by filing an application for the appointment of a guardian for the respondent pursuant to G.S. 35A-1210 or by filing a motion in the cause pursuant to G.S. 35A-1207. The Clerk also may join a person as a party in a pending guardianship proceeding in response to a motion to intervene pursuant to N.C. R. Civ. P. Rule 24.

4.2
Pleadings and Motions

A. Petition and Application

The primary pleadings in a proceeding to appoint a guardian for an allegedly incapacitated adult are the petition and an application for appointment of guardian (which may be joined with or filed subsequent to the filing of the petition). G.S. 35A-1106; G.S. 35A-1210. In most cases, the application for appointment of guardian is included in the petition seeking a determination of the respondent's incapacity.

The North Carolina Administrative Office of the Courts has developed a form (AOC-SP-200) that can be used as the petition and application in guardianship proceedings involving allegedly incapacitated adults.

Verification. G.S. 35A-1105 requires that a petition for the appointment of a guardian for an allegedly incapacitated adult be verified by the petitioner.

Signing. The petition must be signed by the petitioner or, if the petitioner is represented by an attorney, by the petitioner's attorney. N.C. R. Civ. P. Rule 11(a).

Title. As a matter of custom and practice, pleadings in guardianship proceedings generally are titled as "In re [Name of Respondent]," rather than "[Name of Petitioner] v. [Name of Respondent]."

Contents. G.S. 35A-1106 and G.S. 35A-1210 require that a petition for the appointment of a guardian for an allegedly incapacitated adult contain the following information to the extent that it is known to the petitioner:

- the petitioner's name, address, and county of residence;
- the petitioner's interest in the proceeding;
- the respondent's name, age, address, and county of residence;
- the name, address, and county of residence of any person who is the respondent's next of kin or who is known to have an interest in the proceeding;

- the facts that tend to show that the respondent is incapacitated and a statement of the reasons why a determination of the respondent's incapacity and the appointment of a guardian for the respondent are being sought;

- information regarding any adjudication of the respondent's incapacity by a court of another state if the petitioner is seeking a determination of incapacity on the basis of another court's order adjudicating the respondent's incapacity;

- whether the petitioner is seeking the appointment of a general guardian, guardian of the person, or guardian of the estate for the respondent;

- the name of the person, corporation, or disinterested public agent that is recommended as the respondent's guardian; and

- a general statement of the amount or value of the respondent's income, receivables, property, assets, and liabilities.

B. Responsive Pleadings and Motions

G.S. Ch. 35A does not require the respondent, the respondent's attorney, or the respondent's *guardian ad litem* to file an answer or other pleading in response to a petition for the appointment of a guardian. A respondent or the respondent's counsel or *guardian ad litem*, however, may file an answer or motion to dismiss in response to a petition in a guardianship proceeding.

Because G.S. Ch. 35A is silent with respect to answers and motions to dismiss, it is unclear whether a respondent's answer or motion to dismiss must be filed within 10 days after service of the petition pursuant to G.S. 1-394 or whether it may be filed at any time on or before the date of the hearing to determine the respondent's incapacity. If a respondent files an answer or motion to dismiss, it must be served on all of the parties to the proceeding pursuant to N.C. R. Civ. P. Rule 5.

Failure to file an answer or motion to dismiss does not provide a basis for entering default or default judgment against the respondent pursuant to N.C. R. Civ. P. Rule 55.

C. Other Motions and Pleadings

G.S. 35A-1207 allows any "interested person" to file a motion in a pending guardianship proceeding regarding any matter that pertains to the guardianship. *See In re Ward*, 337 N.C. 443 (1994).

4.3
Summons Not Required

In most civil actions and special proceedings, the Clerk of Superior Court issues a summons that must be served on the defendant or respondent pursuant to N.C. R. Civ. P. Rule 4, and notifies the defendant or respondent that if he fails to file a timely answer or response to the complaint or petition, the plaintiff or petitioner will apply to the court for the relief sought in the complaint or petition.

The Clerk's office, however, does *not* issue a summons in a proceeding seeking the appointment of a guardian for an allegedly incapacitated adult. Instead, the notice of hearing issued and served pursuant to G.S. 35A-1108 and G.S. 35A-1109 serves the same function as, and dispenses with any necessity for, a summons. *See In re Barker*, 210 N.C. 617 (1936).

4.4
Notice of Hearing

A. Issuance

G.S. 35A-1108 requires the Clerk to issue a notice of hearing within five days after the petition is filed.

B. Contents

The notice of hearing must state the date, time, and place of the hearing. G.S. 35A-1108.

The North Carolina Administrative Office of the Courts (AOC) has adopted a form (AOC-SP-201) that is used by Clerks to provide notice of hearing in guardianship proceedings. The AOC form also notifies the respondent that a petition has been filed alleging that

- the respondent is incompetent and requesting that a guardian be appointed for the respondent;

- a *guardian ad litem* has been appointed for her;

- she may retain, at her own expense, counsel to represent her in connection with the proceeding; and

- she may file a written response to the petition with the Clerk at or before the time set for the hearing.

C. New Notice of Hearing

If a multidisciplinary evaluation or mediation is ordered after the initial notice of hearing is issued and, as a result, the date for the hearing is continued, the Clerk must issue a new notice advising the parties that the hearing has been continued and stating the reason for the continuance and the date, time, and place of the new hearing. G.S. 35A-1108(b).

4.5
Service of Petition and Notice of Hearing

A. Service on the Respondent

Copies of the petition and the initial notice of hearing must be served on the respondent. G.S. 35A-1109. *See also In re Robinson*, 26 N.C. App. 341 (1975).

Service by sheriff or other authorized person. If the respondent is served in North Carolina, the petition and notice of hearing must be served by the sheriff of the county in which the respondent is served or by some other person duly authorized by law to serve the petition and notice. G.S. 35A-1109; N.C. R. Civ. P. Rule 4(a). If the respondent is served outside North Carolina, the petition and notice may be served by any person who is at least twenty-one years of age, is not a party to the proceeding, and is duly authorized to serve the petition and notice under the law of the state in which service is made. N.C. R. Civ. P. Rule 4(a).

In North Carolina, a sheriff must serve the petition and notice without advance payment of the fee for service. G.S. 35A-1109.

Personal service. Copies of the petition and initial notice of hearing must be served on the respondent by giving them personally to the respondent. G.S. 35A-1109. The petition and initial notice of hearing may *not* be served on the respondent by other means, such as leaving copies of the petition and notice with a person of suitable age and discretion residing at the respondent's dwelling house or usual place of abode, delivering them to the respondent's agent, sending them to the respondent by registered or certified mail or through a designated delivery service or the Postal Service's signature confirmation service, or serving the respondent's counsel or *guardian ad litem.*

Practice Note: The respondent's counsel or *guardian ad litem* may *not* waive personal service of the petition and notice of hearing on the respondent or accept service of the petition and notice of hearing on behalf of the respondent.

Timing of service. The petition and notice must be served on the respondent at least ten days before the date of the hearing regarding the respondent's alleged incapacity. G.S. 35A-1108(a).

Return of service. When the sheriff serves the petition and notice of hearing on the respondent in North Carolina, the sheriff files a return of service (side two of AOC-SP-201) noting the date, time, and address at which the respondent was served.

B. Service on the Respondent's Counsel or *Guardian ad Litem*

G.S. 35A-1109 also requires that the respondent's counsel or *guardian ad litem* be served with the petition and initial notice of hearing pursuant to N.C. R. Civ. P. Rule 4(j).

C. Service on the Respondent's Next of Kin and Other Interested Persons

The petitioner must send copies of the petition and initial notice of hearing to the respondent's next of kin and to any other persons designated by the Clerk by first-class mail within five days after filing the petition and file an affidavit of mailing or certificate of acceptance of notice (AOC-SP-207) with the Clerk. G.S. 35A-1109.

"Next of kin" probably means the person or persons who are most closely related by blood, adoption, or marriage to the respondent (for example, the respondent's spouse or, if the respondent is not married, the respondent's children, or, if the respondent is unmarried and does not have any children, the respondent's parents). *See In re Bry*ant, 116 N.C. App. 329 (1994).

Failure to provide notice of a pending guardianship proceeding to a respondent's next of kin is not a basis for invalidating an order determining the respondent's incapacity or appointing a guardian for the respondent. *See In re Barker*, 210 N.C. 617 (1936). *Cf. In re Ward*, 337 N.C. 443 (1994) (holding that failure to give notice of an adult guardianship proceeding to an "interested person" was a sufficient ground for setting aside the guardianship order on the "interested person's" motion).

4.6
Service of Other Pleadings and Motions

Subsequent notices of hearing, pleadings, and motions must be served on parties to the proceeding, on respondent's counsel or *guardian ad litem*, and on other persons designated by the Clerk. G.S. 35A-1207(c); G.S. 35A-1211.

The Clerk is responsible for sending subsequent hearing notices to the respondent's next of kin and other appropriate persons by first-class mail. G.S. 35A-1109. Except as otherwise provided by law, other notices, pleadings, and motions must be served pursuant to N.C. R. Civ. P. Rule 5, unless the Clerk orders otherwise. G.S. 35A-1108(c); G.S. 35A-1207(c); G.S. 35A-1211(b).

Appendix 4-1
Additional Resources

The North Carolina Administrative Office of the Courts has developed a form (AOC-SP-200) that can be used as the petition and application in guardianship proceedings involving allegedly incapacitated adults. This form is available on line: www.nccourts.org/Forms/Documents/707.pdf.

The North Carolina Administrative Office of the Courts has adopted a form (AOC-SP-201) that is used by Clerks to provide notice of hearing in guardianship proceedings. This form is available on-line: www.nccourts.org/Forms/Documents/669.pdf.

CHAPTER 5:
Hearings, Practice, and Procedure

5.1
Scope of this Chapter

This chapter addresses much, but not all, of the practice and procedure in proceedings for the appointment of a guardian for an incapacitated adult.

Procedures governing the retention of counsel and the appointment of counsel or *guardians ad litem* for allegedly incapacitated respondents are discussed in Chapter 2.

Jurisdiction and venue in guardianship proceedings are discussed in Chapter 3. Parties, pleadings, and notice in guardianship proceedings are discussed in Chapter 4.

Procedures governing the determination of a respondent's incapacity and the appointment of a guardian for an incapacitated adult are discussed in Chapters 6 and 7.

Procedures governing the mediation of guardianship cases are discussed in Chapter 8.

Procedures governing the appeal of orders determining the incapacity of adults and appointing guardians for incapacitated adults are discussed in Chapter 9.

Procedures governing the restoration of a ward's capacity and the modification of guardianship orders are discussed in Chapter 10.

5.2
Nature of Adult Guardianship Proceedings

A. Civil, Not Criminal, Proceedings

Proceedings to appoint a guardian for an incapacitated adult are civil, rather than criminal, in nature. *See In re Dunn*, 239 N.C. 378 (1954). They are, however, *sui generis*.

B. "Quasi" Special Proceedings, Estate Proceedings, and Special Proceedings

Proceedings to appoint a guardian for an incapacitated adult are not considered to be civil actions. *See In re Dunn*, 239 N.C. 378 (1954). And despite the language of G.S. 1-3 (defining any civil proceeding that is not a civil action as a special proceeding), they are not considered to be special proceedings. *See In re Dunn*, 239 N.C. 378 (1954).

Proceedings to appoint a guardian for an incapacitated adult, however, are treated as special proceedings for some purposes. *See In re Dunn*, 239 N.C. 378 (1954); *In re Daniels*, 67 N.C. App. 533 (1984); G.S. 35A-1116(a).

Certain aspects of guardianship proceedings, though, are treated as "estate" matters, rather than special proceedings. *See In re Simmons*, 266 N.C. 702 (1966); *In re Bidstrup*, 55 N.C. App. 394 (1982).

And some proceedings regarding the estates or property of incapacitated wards are expressly designated as special proceedings. *See* G.S. 35A-1301; G.S. 35A-1306; G.S. 35A-1307; G.S. 35A-1310.

5.3
Rules of Procedure

A. Scope of N.C. Rules of Civil Procedure

Rule 1 of the N.C. Rules of Civil Procedure provides that North Carolina's Rules of Civil Procedure "govern the procedure in the superior and district courts . . . in all actions and proceedings of a civil nature except when a differing procedure is prescribed by statute." Similarly, G.S. 1-393 provides that the Rules of Civil Procedure and the provisions of G.S. Ch. 1, Art. 33 apply to special proceedings except as otherwise provided by law.

B. Application of Rules of Civil Procedure to Adult Guardianship Proceedings

Although proceedings to appoint a guardian for an incapacitated adult are not considered to be special proceedings, they are treated as special proceedings for some purposes and they are clearly "proceedings of a civil nature." *See In re Dunn*, 239 N.C. 378 (1954). Moreover, it is clear that these guardianship proceedings, when heard by the Clerk of Superior Court, are proceedings "in superior court." *See* G.S. 7A-40.

It therefore follows that the Rules of Civil Procedure apply to proceedings before the Clerk involving the appointment of guardians for incapacitated adults except to the extent that G.S. Ch. 35A or other statutes prescribe different procedures.

5.4
Right to Jury Trial

A. Constitutional Right to Jury Trial

The provisions of Art. I, Sec. 25 of the North Carolina Constitution, preserving the right to a jury trial in certain civil cases, do not apply to proceedings to appoint a guardian for an incapacitated adult. *See Groves v. Ware*, 182 N.C. 553 (1921); *In re Cook*, 218 N.C. 384 (1940).

B. Statutory Right to Jury Trial

G.S. 35A-1110 gives the respondent the right to a jury trial in a proceeding to appoint a guardian for the respondent.

The respondent's right to a jury trial extends only to the issue of whether the respondent is incompetent or incapacitated and does not extend to issues regarding who should be appointed as the respondent's guardian, the rights that the respondent will be allowed to retain, or the powers that will be granted to the respondent's guardian.

C. Demand for Jury Trial

The respondent's right to a jury trial may be invoked by the respondent or by the respondent's attorney or *guardian ad litem*. G.S. 35A-1110. The petitioner does not have the right to a jury trial on the issue of the respondent's incapacity.

Failure to make a timely request for a jury trial constitutes a waiver of the respondent's right thereto. G.S. 35A-1110. In order to demand a jury trial, the respondent, the respondent's retained counsel, or the respondent's appointed *guardian ad litem* must file the demand with the Clerk and serve it on all parties to the proceeding within 10 days after service of the petition or the last pleading directed to the issue of respondent's incapacity. N.C. R. Civ. P. Rule 38(b), (d).

If the respondent or respondent's counsel or *guardian ad litem* makes a timely demand for a jury trial on the issue of incapacity, the demand may not be withdrawn without the consent of all of the parties to the proceeding. N.C. R. Civ. P. Rule 38(d).

If the respondent fails to make a timely demand for a jury trial, the Clerk, on the Clerk's own motion, may, nonetheless, order a jury trial on the issue of incapacity. G.S. 35A-1110; N.C. R. Civ. P. Rule 39(b).

D. Selection of Jurors

If a jury trial is demanded by the respondent or ordered by the Clerk, the jury is composed of twelve persons chosen from the county's jury list in accordance with the provisions of G.S. Chapter 9 and empaneled pursuant to local rules of practice and procedure. The parties, however, may stipulate that the jury consist of fewer than twelve persons or that a finding on the issue of capacity by a majority of the jurors be taken as the jury's verdict. *See* N.C. R. Civ. P. Rule 48.

E. Jury Instructions

Suggested jury instructions, jury forms, and procedures for jury trials in guardianship proceedings involving allegedly incapacitated adults are included in the *North Carolina Clerk of Superior Court Procedures Manual* (Chapel Hill: School of Government, The University of North Carolina at Chapel Hill, 2003).

F. Hearing Without a Jury

If a jury trial is not demanded by the respondent and is not ordered by the Clerk, the Clerk acts as the finder of fact with respect to the issue of incapacity.

5.5
Voluntary Dismissal, Default Judgment, and Summary Judgment

A. Voluntary Dismissal by Petitioner

A petitioner may voluntarily dismiss, without an order by the Clerk, a proceeding seeking the appointment of a guardian for the respondent pursuant to N.C. R. Civ. P. Rule 41(a)(1). G.S. 35A-1112(g). If, however, the petitioner has filed a motion seeking the appointment of an interim guardian pursuant to G.S. 35A-1114, the petitioner's notice of voluntary dismissal must be filed before the hearing on the motion for appointment of an interim guardian. G.S. 35A-1114(f).

B. Default and Default Judgment

Because G.S. Ch. 35A does not require a respondent to file an answer or other responsive pleading in a proceeding to appoint a guardian for an incapacitated adult, a respondent's failure to file an answer or motion to dismiss does not provide a basis for entering default or default judgment against the respondent pursuant to N.C. R. Civ. P. Rule 55. *See In re Thrift*, 137 N.C. App. 559, 563 (2000) (juvenile proceeding).

C. Summary Judgment

Similarly, summary judgment against a respondent in a proceeding under G.S. Ch. 35A, Art. 1 or Art. 5 is inappropriate. *See In re J.N.S.*, 165 N.C. App. 536 (2004) (juvenile proceeding).

5.6
Discovery

A. G.S. Ch. 35A, N.C. Rules of Civil Procedure, and Local Rules of Practice

G.S. Ch. 35A does not expressly address the issue of discovery in guardianship proceedings and the time frame under G.S. Ch. 35A for hearing and deciding cases involving the appointment of guardians for incapacitated adults renders the application of the discovery procedures under the Rules of Civil Procedure problematic.

Discovery in guardianship proceedings may be addressed through local rules of practice and procedure or in connection with a pre-trial order entered in a pending guardianship proceeding pursuant to N.C. R. Civ. P. Rule 16.

B. Subpoenas

A party or a party's attorney may obtain documents that are relevant to a pending guardianship proceeding through the issuance of a subpoena pursuant to N.C. R. Civ. P. Rule 45.

As the presiding judicial officer in guardianship proceedings, the Clerk may issue subpoenas, compel the production of documents, and issue commissions to take the testimony of witnesses in connection with a pending guardianship proceeding. *See* G.S. 7A-103(1), (3).

C. Discovery of Medical Records

Obtaining medical records and health information regarding an allegedly incapacitated respondent is problematic because this information may be privileged or confidential under federal and state laws (such as G.S. 8-53 and the federal medical privacy rules adopted pursuant to the Health Insurance Portability and Protection Act) that restrict the disclosure of this information. And unlike a *guardian ad litem* appointed to represent a juvenile in a juvenile proceeding involving abuse, neglect, or dependency (*see* G.S. 7B-601(c)), a *guardian ad litem* appointed to represent an allegedly incapacitated respondent under G.S. 35A-1107 does *not* have a statutory right to obtain medical records, health information, or other information that is privileged or confidential unless the subject of the information consents, the disclosure is authorized by law, or a court orders disclosure of the information.

5.7
Pre-Trial Conference

Although G.S. Ch. 35A does not include provisions for pre-trial conferences in guardianship proceedings, the Clerk may hold a pre-trial conference and enter a pre-trial order in a guardianship proceeding pursuant to N.C. R. Civ. P. Rule 16.

5.8
Appointment of Interim Guardian

An interim guardian is a temporary guardian who is appointed pursuant to G.S. 35A-1114 to protect an allegedly incapacitated respondent's well-being or estate from imminent harm before a judicial determination of the respondent's incapacity.

Practice Note: G.S. 35A-1114 does not authorize the appointment of an "interim" or "emergency" guardian after the Clerk has determined that a respondent is incapacitated and has appointed a guardian for the respondent—even in cases in which there is an emergency due to the guardian's death, resignation, removal, or failure or refusal to protect the ward. The Clerk, however, may enter an emergency order under G.S. 35A-1291 to protect the ward or the ward's property in these situations.

A. Motion for Appointment

A petitioner may seek the appointment of an interim guardian at the same time that he or she files a petition for adjudication of the respondent's incompetence or at any time subsequent to the filing of such a petition. G.S. 35A-1114(a). A request for appointment of an interim guardian is made by filing a verified motion setting forth facts that tend to show that

- there is reasonable cause to believe that the respondent is incapacitated, *and*

- intervention is required to protect the respondent's physical well-being or the respondent's estate from an imminent or foreseeable risk of harm, *and*

- immediate appointment of an interim guardian for the respondent or the respondent's estate is required. G.S. 35A-1114(a), (b).

B.   Notice of Hearing

Upon the filing of a motion for the appointment of an interim guardian, the Clerk must immediately set a date, time, and place for a hearing on the motion. G.S. 35A-1114(c). The motion and notice of hearing must be served on the respondent, the respondent's attorney or *guardian ad litem*, and any other persons designated by the Clerk. G.S. 35A-1114(c).

C.   Hearing

A hearing on the motion for appointment of an interim guardian must be held as soon as possible, but no later than 15 days after the motion has been served on the respondent. G.S. 35A-1114(c).

D.   Order Appointing Interim Guardian

The Clerk is required to appoint an interim guardian for the respondent or the respondent's estate if, after the hearing, the Clerk determines that

- there is reasonable cause to believe that the respondent is incapacitated, *and*

- there is an imminent or foreseeable risk of harm to the respondent's physical well-being and an immediate need for a guardian to provide consent or take other steps to protect the respondent, *or* there is an imminent or foreseeable risk of harm to the respondent's estate and immediate intervention is required to protect the respondent's interests. G.S. 35A-1114(d).

The Clerk's order appointing an interim guardian must contain specific findings of fact to support the Clerk's conclusions regarding the respondent's probable incapacity and the need for an interim guardian. G.S. 35A-1114(e).

E.   Qualifications and Authority of Interim Guardian

G.S. 35A-1114 does not directly address the qualifications of an interim guardian. An interim guardian whose authority relates only to the person of a respondent is not required to post a bond. If the interim guardian is granted authority with respect to the respondent's estate, the interim guardian must post a bond in an amount and subject to any conditions determined by the Clerk. G.S. 35A-1114(e).

The powers and duties of the interim guardian must be set forth in the Clerk's order and must be limited to those necessary to meet the conditions necessitating appointment of the interim guardian. G.S. 35A-1114(e). An interim guardian's authority terminates upon the earliest of the following conditions:

- the date specified in the Clerk's order;

- 45 days from the date of the Clerk's order (unless extended, for good cause, by the Clerk for an additional period of 45 days);

- the appointment of a guardian for the respondent or the respondent's estate pursuant to G.S. Ch. 35A, Art. 5;

- the dismissal of the incompetency petition by the Clerk. G.S. 35A-1114(e).

5.9
Order for Multidisciplinary Evaluation

A. Nature and Purpose of Multidisciplinary Evaluations

A multidisciplinary evaluation (MDE) is an evaluation that is prepared by a designated human services agency at the direction of the Clerk of Superior Court pursuant to G.S. 35A-1111 regarding the nature and extent of a respondent's or ward's incapacity. The purpose of an MDE is to assist the Clerk in determining whether or to what extent the respondent is incapacitated, whether a limited guardianship is appropriate, or other issues regarding guardianship.

An MDE must include current (within the past year) medical, psychological, and social work evaluations as directed by the Clerk and may include evaluations by other professionals regarding the respondent's or ward's needs with respect to education, vocational rehabilitation, occupational therapy, vocational therapy, psychiatry, speech therapy, etc. G.S. 35A-1101(14). Suggested guidelines for the preparation of MDEs in incompetency proceedings have been developed by the North Carolina Department of Health and Human Services' Division of Aging and Adult Services.

B. Motion for Multidisciplinary Evaluations

G.S. Ch. 35A does not require that an MDE be prepared in every guardianship proceeding involving an allegedly incapacitated respondent.

Instead, G.S. 35A-1111 and G.S. 35A-1212(b) allow the Clerk, on his or her own motion or on the motion of any party, to order an MDE of a respondent or ward in an adult guardianship proceeding.

A party's request for an MDE must be filed with the Clerk within 10 days after service of the petition on the respondent. G.S. 35A-1111(a). North Carolina's Administrative Office of the Courts has developed a model form for the Request and Order for Multidisciplinary Evaluation (AOC-SP-901M).

C. Order for Multidisciplinary Evaluation

Although ordering an MDE is within the Clerk's discretion, the Clerk should order an MDE, even in the absence of a request by a party, when there is insufficient or conflicting evidence regarding the respondent's alleged incapacity, when it appears that limited guardianship may be appropriate, or when additional information is needed in order to develop an appropriate guardianship plan.

The Clerk's order for an MDE may require the respondent to attend the MDE for the purpose of being evaluated. G.S. 35A-1111(d). If the respondent *willfully* fails to attend the MDE as ordered by the Clerk, the respondent may be held in civil or criminal contempt in accordance with the procedures specified in G.S. Ch. 5A. The Clerk, however, does not have any express or inherent authority to order law enforcement officers to enforce the Clerk's order by seizing the respondent and transporting him or her to the evaluation. *See In re Transportation of Juveniles*, 102 N.C. App. 806 (1991).

D. Filing of Multidisciplinary Evaluation

If an MDE is ordered, the designated agency is required to file the evaluation with the Clerk and, unless otherwise ordered by the Clerk, to send copies of the evaluation to the petitioner, the respondent's *guardian ad litem*, and the respondent's retained counsel within 30 days from the date the agency receives the Clerk's order to perform the evaluation. G.S. 35A-1111(b).

If the evaluation does not include the medical, psychological, or social work evaluations ordered by the Clerk, the agency nonetheless must file and serve the evaluation along with an explanation as to why the evaluation does not contain the required medical, psychological, or social work evaluations. G.S. 35A-1111(c).

An MDE is not a public record and its contents may not be revealed, released, or disclosed except by order of the Clerk. G.S. 35A-1111(b). The Administrative Office of the Courts suggests that the copy of the MDE that is filed with the Clerk be placed in the court file in a sealed envelope marked "Multidisciplinary Evaluation: Do Not Open."

An MDE may be considered by the court at a hearing to determine the respondent's incapacity or to appoint a guardian for an incapacitated respondent. G.S. 35A-1111(e).

5.10
Calendaring and Continuance of Hearings

The hearing on a petition to appoint a guardian for an allegedly incapacitated adult must be held not less than 10, nor more than 30, days after service of the petition and notice of hearing on the respondent, unless the clerk extends the time for the hearing in order to complete mediation of the issues, for preparation of a multidisciplinary evaluation, or for other good cause. G.S. 35A-1108(a).

If the Clerk orders a multidisciplinary evaluation after the initial notice of hearing has been issued, the Clerk may extend the time for the hearing, which must be held not less than 10, nor more than 30, days after service of the second hearing notice on the respondent. G.S. 35A-1108(b).

5.11
Hearing Procedure

Practice Note: Suggested hearing procedures for guardianship proceedings involving allegedly incapacitated adults are included in the *North Carolina Clerk of Superior Court Procedures Manual* (Chapel Hill: School of Government, The University of North Carolina at Chapel Hill, 2003).

This section discusses adult guardianship hearings before the Clerk of Superior Court. In guardianship proceedings that are heard before a Superior Court Judge pursuant to G.S. 35A-1103(d) or G.S. 35A-1115, the Superior Court Judge, rather than the Clerk of Superior Court, exercises the judicial authority and functions described below, unless otherwise specified.

A. The Clerk's Role and Responsibilities

The Clerk of Superior Court or an Assistant Clerk of Superior Court presides as the judge in a hearing regarding the appointment of a guardian for an allegedly incapacitated respondent under G.S. Ch. 35A, Arts. 1 and 5. As the presiding judicial officer in guardianship proceedings, the Clerk has the authority to administer oaths and to preserve order in his or her court. *See* G.S. 7A-103(2), (7).

Unless a jury is empaneled to determine the issue of the respondent's incapacity, the Clerk is the trier of fact and may not transfer a contested guardianship proceeding for hearing by a Superior Court Judge. G.S. 1-301.2(g)(1).

B. Open and Closed Hearings

The hearing regarding appointment of a guardian for an allegedly incapacitated adult is open to the public unless the respondent, the respondent's retained counsel, or the respondent's *guardian ad litem* requests that the hearing be closed. G.S. 35A-1112(a). The hearing may not be closed on the motion of the petitioner or on the Clerk's own motion. If the respondent requests that the hearing be closed, the Clerk must exclude all persons other than those directly involved in or testifying at the hearing.

C. Sequestering Witnesses

The Clerk may, at the request of a party or on the Clerk's own motion, exclude witnesses so that they cannot hear the testimony of other witnesses, but may not exclude a natural person who is a party to the proceeding, an officer or employee of a party that is not a natural person if the officer or employee has been designated by the party's attorney as the party's representative, a person whose presence is necessary to a party, or a person whose presence is in the interest of justice. N.C. R. Evid. Rule 615.

D. Presence of the Respondent

Although the respondent has the right to attend the hearing, the respondent's presence is not required.

Practice Note: The attorney who is appointed as the respondent's *guardian ad litem* should make reasonable efforts to ensure that the respondent is present at an adult guardianship hearing unless the respondent's attendance at the hearing would jeopardize the respondent's physical, mental, or medical condition or otherwise be contrary to the respondent's best interest. In some cases, it may be appropriate to ask the Clerk to conduct all or part of an adult guardianship hearing at the location where the respondent resides.

E. Right to Present Evidence

The petitioner and the respondent are entitled to present testimony and documentary evidence, to subpoena witnesses and the production of documents, and to examine and cross-examine witnesses. G.S. 35A-1112(b). Although the respondent's next of kin and other interested persons do not have the right to present evidence, examine and cross-examine witnesses, make arguments to the court, or otherwise participate in a guardianship hearing, the Clerk may allow them to do so.

F. Issues of Fact and Law

Proceedings under G.S. Ch. 35A, Arts. 1 and 5 involve two primary issues:

- whether the respondent is an incapacitated adult;
- if so, who should be appointed as the respondent's guardian.

Guardianship proceedings under G.S. Ch. 35A, Arts. 1 and 5, however, also involve related and overlapping issues regarding

- the nature and extent of the respondent's incapacity;
- whether a general guardian, guardian of the person, or guardian of the estate should be appointed;
- whether a limited guardianship is appropriate;
- what rights should be retained by the respondent; and
- to what extent the guardian's powers should be limited.

G. Bifurcated Hearings

In a proceeding involving the appointment of a guardian for an allegedly incapacitated adult, the court does not reach or decide issues regarding whether a guardian should be appointed, whether the guardianship should be limited, and who should be appointed as the respondent's guardian unless the court first determines that the respondent is an incapacitated adult.

Because issues regarding the appointment of a guardian are contingent upon a determination that the respondent is incapacitated and because the issues of incapacity and appointment of guardians for incapacitated adults are addressed separately in two different articles of G.S. Ch. 35A, some Clerks bifurcate hearings involving the appointment of guardians for incapacitated adults, hearing and determining the issue of the respondent's incapacity first, and then hearing and determining issues regarding who should be appointed as the respondent's guardian and whether a limited guardianship is appropriate. G.S. Ch. 35A, however, does not require that guardianship proceedings be bifurcated in this manner.

H. Recording Hearings

Because the Superior Court conducts a *de novo* hearing on the issue of a respondent's incapacity if the Clerk's order determining incapacity under G.S. Ch. 35A, Art. 1 is appealed, the Clerk is not required to record that portion of a bifurcated guardianship proceeding involving the respondent's incapacity. The Clerk, however, is required, upon request of a party, to make an electronic recording of the portion of a bifurcated guardianship proceeding involving the appointment of a guardian for a respondent who has been adjudicated incompetent. G.S. 1-301.3(f). When a guardianship proceeding is not bifurcated, the entire proceeding should be recorded.

5.12
Evidentiary Issues and Burden of Proof

A. Application of N.C. Rules of Evidence in Adult Guardianship Proceedings

The North Carolina Rules of Evidence apply to proceedings involving the appointment of guardians for incapacitated persons. N.C. R. Evid. Rule 1101.

B. Consideration of Improperly Admitted Evidence

When a judge hears a case without a jury, the law presumes that the judge will disregard improperly admitted evidence and that the improper admission of evidence is not prejudicial. *See State v. Cheek*, 307 N.C. 552 (1983); *Pritchard v. Pritchard*, 45 N.C. App. 189 (1980). This presumption, however, does not apply if there is a timely and proper objection to the evidence, the judge erroneously overrules the objection, and a party properly assigns error to the judge's ruling on appeal. *See Douglas v. W.C. Mallison & Son*, 265 N.C. 362 (1965); *Carson v. Reid*, 76 N.C. App. 321, *aff'd*, 316 N.C. 189 (1985).

C. Burden of Presenting Evidence

The petitioner has the burden of presenting evidence sufficient to prove that the respondent is an incapacitated adult and, if the petitioner is requesting that the petitioner or another person be appointed as the respondent's guardian, presenting evidence regarding the proposed guardian's qualification and suitability.

D. Mode and Order of Presenting Evidence

The Clerk has the authority to control the mode and order of interrogation and presentation of evidence as provided in N.C. R. Evid. Rule 611.

All testimony in proceedings involving the appointment of a guardian for an incapacitated adult must be offered under oath or affirmation. N.C. R. Evid. Rule 603.

The Clerk may, on the Clerk's own motion or at the suggestion of a party, call witnesses. N.C. R. Evid. Rule 614(a). The Clerk also may question witnesses called by a party or called by the court. N.C. R. Evid. Rule 614(b).

E. Hearsay

"Hearsay" is a statement, other than one made by the declarant while testifying at the hearing, that is offered in evidence to prove the truth of the matter asserted. N.C. R. Evid. Rule 801(c). Upon proper objection by a party, the Clerk must refuse to admit or consider hearsay evidence in a proceeding involving the appointment of a guardian for an incapacitated adult except as provided by statute or the Rules of Evidence. N.C. R. Evid. Rule 802.

F. Physician-Patient Privilege

Communications between the respondent and the respondent's doctor, information obtained by the respondent's doctor in connection with the doctor's treatment of the respondent, and information in medical records regarding the medical treatment of or health care provided to the respondent are privileged and protected from disclosure in connection with legal proceedings. G.S. 8-53.

This privilege, however, may be waived expressly by the respondent, the respondent's counsel, or the respondent's *guardian ad litem* and is implicitly waived if

- the respondent or the respondent's counsel or *guardian ad litem* fails to object to the admissibility of otherwise privileged testimony or evidence;

- the respondent or the respondent's counsel or *guardian ad litem* calls the respondent's doctor as a witness and examines the doctor with respect to the respondent's medical condition;

- the respondent testifies regarding communications between the respondent and the respondent's doctor; or

- the respondent or the respondent's counsel or *guardian ad litem* directly places the respondent's medical condition at issue. *See Mims v. Wright*, 157 N.C. App. 339 (2003).

If the respondent or the respondent's counsel or *guardian ad litem* has not waived the patient-physician privilege, the Clerk may order that otherwise admissible privileged or confidential information regarding the respondent's medical condition or treatment be admitted in evidence upon a finding that disclosure of the information is necessary for the proper administration of justice. G.S. 8-53.

G. Medical Records

Medical records regarding the respondent's medical condition or treatment may be admitted as evidence in a proceeding to appoint a guardian for an incapacitated adult if

- the respondent or the respondent's counsel or *guardian ad litem* stipulates or fails to object to their admission in evidence; or

- the records are relevant (N.C. R. Evid. Rule 401); are properly authenticated (N.C. R. Evid. Rule 901); are admissible under the "business record" exception to the hearsay rule (N.C. R. Evid. Rule 803(6)) or another exception to the hearsay rule; and the respondent or the respondent's counsel or *guardian ad litem* has waived the physician-patient privilege with respect to the records or the Clerk has ordered that the records be disclosed under G.S. 8-53.

H. Multidisciplinary Evaluation (MDE)

G.S. 35A-1111(e) provides that an MDE may be considered by the Clerk at a hearing regarding the respondent's incapacity, at a hearing regarding the appointment of a guardian for an incapacitated respondent, or both.

I. Opinion Testimony by Lay Witnesses

A witness who has not been qualified to testify as an expert witness may offer his or her opinion regarding a respondent's mental incapacity if the lay witness's opinion is rationally based on the witness's perception of the respondent and the Clerk determines that the witness's opinion regarding the respondent's incapacity will be helpful in understanding the witness's testimony or determining the respondent's incapacity. N.C. R. Evid. Rule 701. *See State v. Strickland*, 321 N.C. 31 (1987); *State v. Davis*, 321 N.C. 52 (1987); *State v. Bond*, 345 N.C. 1 (1996).

J. Testimony by Experts

If a witness is properly qualified as an expert witness, he or she may testify regarding his or her opinion regarding the respondent's capacity to manage the respondent's affairs or to make or communicate important decisions regarding the respondent's person, family, or property. N.C. R. Evid. Rule 704. *See State v. Shank*, 322 N.C. 243 (1988). *See also* N.C. R. Evid. Rules 702, 703, 705, 706.

K. Testimony by the Respondent

The respondent may be called by the petitioner, by the respondent's counsel or *guardian ad litem*, by any other party, or by the Clerk to testify as a witness and must testify if he or she is called as a witness and is competent to testify as a witness.

An allegedly incapacitated respondent is competent to testify unless the court determines that he or she lacks the capacity to understand his or her oath as a witness or lacks the capacity to relate the facts that are the subject of his or her testimony. *See In re Will of Leonard*, 82 N.C. App. 646 (1986).

L. Testimony by Respondent's Attorney or Guardian ad litem

Communications between a respondent and the respondent's attorney are generally protected by the attorney-client privilege and, if they are protected by the attorney-client privilege and the privilege has not been waived by the respondent, the respondent's attorney may not testify or be compelled by the court to testify with respect to those communications. *See State v. McIntosh*, 336 N.C. 517, 523 (1994); *In re Miller*, 357 N.C. 316 (2003).

Rule 1.6 of the North Carolina State Bar's Revised Rules of Professional Conduct also prohibits the respondent's lawyer from disclosing other information obtained during the attorney's representation of the respondent unless the respondent gives informed consent to the disclosure, the disclosure is impliedly authorized in connection with the lawyer's representation of the respondent, or the disclosure is required by court order, law, or the Revised Rules of Professional Conduct. These rules do not apply to a lawyer who is appointed as the respondent's *guardian ad litem* if the lawyer is acting solely as the respondent's *guardian ad litem* and not as the respondent's attorney. *See* 2004 Formal Ethics Opinion 11. *See also In re Shepard*, 162 N.C. App. 215 (2004).

M. Presumption of Mental Capacity

The law presumes that, in the absence of proof to the contrary, all adults have sufficient mental capacity to make their own decisions regarding their personal affairs. *See State v. Thompson*, 328 N.C. 477 (1991); *Ridings v. Ridings*, 55 N.C. App. 630 (1982); *In re Womack*, 53 N.C. App. 221 (1981); *State v. Jones*, 293 N.C. 413 (1977); *Hagins v. Greensboro Redevelopment Comm'n*, 275 N.C. 90 (1969) (presumption implicit in holding); *Jones v. Winstead*, 186 N.C. 536 (1923); *Hudson v. Hudson*, 144 N.C. 449 (1907). This presumption, however, may be rebutted by sufficient, competent evidence of mental incapacity in a legal proceeding, including a guardianship proceeding pursuant to G.S. Ch. 35A, in which an adult's mental capacity is at issue.

A finding that a respondent lacks the capacity to consent to protective services made by a district court judge in a special proceeding under G.S. Ch. 108A, Art. 6 is inadmissible and may not be considered in a guardianship proceeding under G.S. Ch. 35A, Art. 1 or 5. G.S. 108A-105(d).

A certified copy of an order entered by a court of another state that includes a finding that a respondent is incompetent may be admissible in a guardianship proceeding under G.S. Ch. 35A, Art. 1 or 5, but it is not necessarily conclusive on the issue of the respondent's incapacity. G.S. 35A-1113.

N. Burden of Proof (Persuasion)

The petitioner has the burden of persuading the Clerk or jury, by clear, cogent, and convincing evidence, that the respondent is incapacitated. *See* G.S. 35A-1112(d). If the petitioner fails to prove the respondent's incapacity by clear, cogent, and convincing evidence, the Clerk must dismiss the proceeding. G.S. 35A-1112(c).

5.13
Findings and Order

A. Order of Dismissal

If the Clerk (or a jury) determines that the respondent is not incapacitated, the Clerk must enter an order dismissing the proceeding.

B. Order and Findings Regarding Incapacity

If the Clerk (or a jury) determines that the respondent is incapacitated, the Clerk must enter an order adjudicating the respondent incompetent. G.S. 35A-1112(d). The Clerk's order should include findings regarding the nature and extent of the respondent's incapacity. *See* G.S. 35A-1112(d).

If the Clerk enters an order adjudicating the respondent incompetent, the Clerk must also enter an order appointing a general guardian, guardian of the person, or guardian of the estate for the respondent (unless the Clerk transfers the case to another county for the appointment of a guardian for the respondent). G.S. 35A-1112(e); G.S. 35A-1215. The Clerk's order appointing a guardian for the respondent may be combined with the Clerk's order adjudicating the respondent incompetent.

C. Order Appointing Guardian

The Clerk's order appointing a guardian for an incapacitated respondent must specify the nature of the guardianship or guardianships to be created, the name of the person or entity that is appointed as the respondent's guardian, the identity of any agency that will serve as the designated agency pursuant to G.S. 35A-1243, and the powers and duties of the guardian or guardians. G.S. 35A-1215(a).

The Clerk's order should contain findings sufficient to support the Clerk's determination that the guardian appointed for the respondent is qualified and suitable to serve as the respondent's guardian.

D. "Limited Guardianship" Orders

The Clerk's order should create a limited guardianship whenever a limited guardianship is appropriate. *See* G.S. 35A-1212(a). If the Clerk orders a limited guardianship, the Clerk's order must include findings regarding the nature and extent of the respondent's incapacity as they relate to the respondent's need for a guardian. G.S. 35A-1215(b). When the Clerk orders a limited guardianship, the Clerk's order may provide that the ward retains certain legal rights and privileges to which the respondent was entitled before he or she was adjudicated incompetent. G.S. 35A-1215(b).

5.14
Costs and Fees

A. Statutory Authority

G.S. 35A-1116 governs the taxing of costs and fees in guardianship proceedings.

B. Order Appointing Guardian for a Ward Who Is Not Indigent

If the court enters an order appointing a guardian for an incapacitated ward who is not
indigent, the Clerk must assess the cost of the respondent's *guardian ad litem*, witness fees,
and the cost of the MDE (if an MDE was prepared) against the respondent, and may tax
the reasonable fees of the petitioner's attorney, the court filing fee, fees for service of process,
and other costs allowed under G.S. 7A-307 or common law against the respondent or the
petitioner.

C. Order Appointing Guardian for a Ward Who Is Indigent

If the court enters an order appointing a guardian for an incapacitated ward and the ward
is indigent, the Clerk may not tax costs and fees against the respondent. In those cases, the
reasonable fee of the respondent's *guardian ad litem* must be paid by the State, witness fees
must be paid by the Administrative Office of the Courts, and the cost of an MDE (if an
MDE was prepared) must be paid by the state Department of Health and Human Services.
Other costs and fees may be taxed against the petitioner.

D. Order Dismissing Petition

If the Clerk finds that the petitioner did not have reasonable grounds to bring the
proceeding, the Clerk must tax the reasonable fees of the respondent's *guardian ad litem*
(but not the reasonable fees of the respondent's retained counsel except as otherwise
provided under N.C. R. Civ. P. Rule 11), witness fees, the cost of the MDE (if an MDE
was prepared), and others costs as allowed by G.S. 7A-307 and the common law against the
petitioner.

   If the Clerk does not enter an order appointing a guardian for the respondent but
finds that the petitioner had reasonable grounds to bring the proceeding, the cost of the
respondent's *guardian ad litem* must be paid by the State, witness fees must be paid by the
Administrative Office of the Courts, and the cost of the MDE (if an MDE was prepared)
must be taxed against the petitioner or the respondent or paid by the state Department
of Health and Human Services. The Clerk may tax the reasonable fees of the petitioner's
attorney, the court filing fee, fees for service of process, and other costs allowed under G.S.
7A-307 or common law against the respondent or the petitioner.

E. Costs and Fees for Mediated Cases

Payment of costs and fees for mediation is discussed in Chapter 8.

Appendix 5-1
Additional Resources

Suggested guidelines for the preparation of MDEs multidisciplinary evaluations in incompetency proceedings have been developed by the North Carolina Department of Health and Human Services' Division of Aging and Adult Services and are available on-line: http://info.dhhs.state.nc.us/olm/manuals/doa/gs/man/AFSc8xg.htm#P9_13.

Suggested jury instructions, jury forms, and procedures for jury trials in guardianship proceedings involving allegedly incapacitated adults are included in the *North Carolina Clerk of Superior Court Procedures Manual* (Chapel Hill: School of Government, The University of North Carolina at Chapel Hill, 2003).

CHAPTER 6:
Incapacity

6.1
Incapacity and Adult Guardianship

A guardian may not be appointed for an adult unless the adult has been adjudicated to be incapacitated or "incompetent" pursuant to G.S. Ch. 35A, Art. 1. *In re Efird*, 114 N.C. App. 638 (1994).

The question of the respondent's "incapacity" or "incompetency," therefore, is a necessary issue and must be determined in any proceeding seeking the appointment of a guardian for the respondent.

6.2
Defining Incapacity

A. Purpose

The legal definition of "incapacity" or "incompetency" is important because it defines the circumstances under which the State may restrict an adult's decision-making authority by appointing a guardian to make personal or financial decisions for him or her.

B. History

Although the concept of mental incapacity or incompetency has always been central in connection with adult guardianship proceedings, there is no, and never has been any, uniform definition of "incapacity" or "incompetency."

Before 1977, North Carolina's guardianship laws, like those of other states, defined "incapacity" or "incompetency" primarily through general, and usually undefined, terms regarding an individual's status, mental incapacity, or condition, including "lunatic," "idiot," "inebriate," "imbecile," "feeble-minded," "mentally deficient," and "insane."

Over the past forty years, however, the national trend generally has been to abandon definitions that rely on pejorative labels (such as "idiot" and "lunatic") in favor of definitions that focus on an individual's mental or physical condition and cognitive and functional impairments.

Historically, legal definitions of "incapacity" or "incompetency" in adult guardianship proceedings have focused on an individual's "global" or general capacity to make decisions or manage his or her property and personal affairs, rather than a person's mental capacity to make decisions with respect to particular transactions or matters, such as marrying, entering into a contract, making a will, standing trial in a criminal proceeding, etc. *See Hagins v. Greensboro Redevelopment Comm'n*, 275 N.C. 90 (1969). More importantly, "incapacity" or "incompetency" in the context of adult guardianship proceedings generally was considered to be "all or nothing." A person either was, or was not, "incapacitated" or "incompetent" and a judicial determination of "incapacity" or "incompetency" generally resulted in a comprehensive, if not almost total, loss of an "incompetent" person's legal rights.

Today, "capacity" and "incapacity" generally are seen to be the two ends of a continuum that includes varying degrees of capacity and incapacity rather than a clearly-differentiated dichotomy—concepts that are more "gray" than "black or white." As a result, many state guardianship laws expressly or implicitly incorporate the concepts of "partial incapacity" and "limited guardianship" into their definitions of "incapacity" or "incompetency."

C. Contemporary Definitional Components

Today, most state adult guardianship laws define "incapacity" or "incompetency" through a combination of two or more of the following components:

- a "medical" component that requires that the respondent's incapacity be caused by a diagnosed medical condition or identified mental or physical impairment, such as mental illness, developmental disability, or chronic intoxication;

- a "functional" component that requires that the respondent's incapacity limit his or her ability to manage his or her own affairs or property or to care for his or her essential personal needs such as medical care, food, clothing, shelter, and safety;

- a "cognitive" component that requires that the respondent's incapacity involve a mental or physical condition that limits his or her ability to make or communicate "rational" decisions;

- a "necessity" component that requires that the respondent's incapacity endanger the respondent's person or property to such an extent that appointment of a guardian, as opposed to some other "less restrictive" alternative, is necessary and in the respondent's best interest.

The 1997 Uniform Guardianship and Protective Proceedings Act, for example, employs the second, third, and fourth components (but not the first component) of "incapacity" in defining an "incapacitated person" as a person "who, for reasons other than being a minor, is unable to receive and evaluate information or make or communicate decisions to such an extent that [he or she] lacks the ability to meet [his or her essential needs with respect to] physical health, safety, or self-care, even with appropriate technological assistance."

6.3
Statutory Definition of Incapacity

G.S. 35A-1101(7) defines an "incompetent adult" as an adult or emancipated minor who

- lacks sufficient capacity to manage his or her own affairs or to make or communicate important decisions concerning his or her person, family, or property,

- due to mental illness, mental retardation, epilepsy, cerebral palsy, autism, inebriety, senility, disease, injury, or similar cause or condition.

Similarly, G.S. 35A-1101(8) defines an "incompetent child" as an unemancipated minor who is at least 17½ years old and, for reasons other than his or her minority, lacks sufficient capacity to manage his or her own affairs or to make or communicate important decisions concerning his or her person, family, or property due to mental illness, mental retardation, epilepsy, cerebral palsy, autism, inebriety, senility, disease, injury, or similar cause or condition.

6.4
Analyzing and Interpreting the Statutory Definition of Incapacity

A. Definitional Components or Elements

North Carolina's definition of incapacity consists of two separate, but related, components or elements:

- a functional or cognitive element; and
- a medical component.

Functional or cognitive element. The functional or cognitive element of the definition refers to an individual's inability to manage his or her affairs or to make or communicate important decisions regarding his or her person, family, or property.

Medical component. The medical component of incapacity refers to the mental or physical condition that is the cause of the individual's inability to make or communicate important decisions or manage his or her affairs.

Relationship between the components or elements. Both components or elements of the definition are necessary in determining the issue of a respondent's incapacity, but neither is sufficient standing alone. The mere fact that a respondent is "mentally ill," for example, is not sufficient, in and of itself, to support a judicial determination that he or she is incapacitated or "incompetent." Instead, the petitioner must prove and the court must find that

- a respondent is mentally ill (or suffers from another mental or physical condition) *and*
- he or she lacks sufficient capacity to manage his or her own affairs or property or to make or communicate important decisions concerning his or her person, family, or property.

In addition, the two components or elements of North Carolina's definition of incapacity are causally related. A respondent's functional or cognitive incapacity must be caused by his or her mental illness, mental retardation, epilepsy, cerebral palsy, autism, inebriety, senility, disease, injury, or similar cause or condition.

B. Minimal or Sufficient vs. Optimal Capacity

It is important to note that North Carolina's definition of incapacity uses the term "sufficient capacity." This strongly suggests that even if a respondent suffers from a cognitive impairment that limits his or her ability to make or communicate important decisions or manage his or her affairs or property, he or she should not be determined to be "incompetent" unless he or she lacks the understanding or mental capacity that is *minimally* required to manage his or her affairs or property. Proof that a respondent's decision-making ability is not optimal or perfect, therefore, is insufficient to support a judicial determination of incapacity under G.S. Ch. 35A, Art. 1. Or, phrased differently, a judicial determination of incapacity requires proof that a respondent's decision-making capacity is *significantly* impaired.

C. Partial Incapacity and Limited Guardianship

It is also important to note that North Carolina's definition of incapacity implicitly incorporates the concepts of "partial incapacity" and "limited guardianship." G.S. 35A-1212 and G.S. 35A-1215 authorize the Clerk to make findings regarding the "nature and extent" of a respondent's incapacity and to create a limited guardianship if a limited guardianship is warranted by the nature and extent of the ward's incapacity. Moreover, G.S. 35A-1201(a)(5) recognizes that, in at least some instances, an "incompetent" ward may retain sufficient capacity to exercise certain rights or make or participate in certain decisions.

D. Temporary and Permanent Incapacity

North Carolina's guardianship law, like that of other states, does not require that a respondent's incapacity be permanent rather than temporary, curable, or reversible. The Clerk's authority, under G.S. 35A-1212 and G.S. 35A-1215, to make findings regarding the "nature and extent" of a respondent's incapacity clearly includes the authority to make findings regarding the probable duration of the respondent's incapacity or prognosis for improvement. If the ward's condition improves, the Clerk may modify the guardianship order and create a limited guardianship if a limited guardianship is warranted given the nature and extent of the ward's incapacity. *See* G.S. 35A-1207. And if the ward's condition improves to the extent that he or she is no longer incompetent, the Clerk is required, upon motion by the ward, the guardian, or an interested party, to enter an order restoring the ward's competency. G.S. 35A-1130.

E. The "Necessity" Component

Although North Carolina's definition of incapacity does not expressly incorporate a "necessity" component, G.S. 35A-1201(a)(4) may implicitly do so by providing that the Clerk should not appoint a guardian for an incompetent respondent unless it is clear that appointing a guardian for the respondent will give the respondent a fuller capacity for exercising his or her rights.

6.5
The Medical Component of Incapacity

The medical component of incapacity refers to a diagnosed medical condition or identified mental or physical condition that is the cause of a respondent's cognitive impairment or functional incapacity.

A. Purpose

The purpose of the medical component of incapacity is to limit the State's authority by providing an objective, medical standard that differentiates between individuals who lack the mental capacity required to act in their own interest and those who are mentally competent but *choose* to act in eccentric, unreasonable, irrational, foolish, crazy, or even self-destructive ways.

Whether definitions of incapacity that require proof of a disabling medical condition or physical or mental impairment actually accomplish this purpose is open to question, especially in light of the fact that at least sixteen states, including North Carolina, have adopted "catch-all" provisions that include the category "other cause" in addition to specified conditions such as "mental illness" and "developmental disability." At least one commentator, therefore, has suggested that the medical component of incapacity "has become superfluous as a definitional standard in the law of guardianship," that it should be abandoned because it has provided only "an aura of objectivity without substance," and that it should be replaced by definitional standards that focus on the cognitive capacity and functional impairments of respondents. *See* Charles P. Sabatino and Suzanna L. Basinger, *Competency: Reforming Our Legal Fictions*, 6 J. Mental Health & Aging 119 (2000).

B. History

The medical component of North Carolina's definition of incapacity was first adopted in 1977, was made generally applicable to all adult guardianship proceedings in 1987, and remains a part of the current statutory definition of incapacity under G.S. 35A-1101(7).

C. Definitions

North Carolina's guardianship statute defines several of the medical diagnoses or mental or physical conditions that comprise the medical component of North Carolina's definition of incapacity.

- "Mental illness" is, and has been since 1945, defined as any "illness that so lessens the capacity of a person to use self-control, judgment, and discretion in the conduct of the person's affairs and social relations as to make it necessary or advisable for the person to be under treatment, care, supervision, guidance, or control." G.S. 35A-1101(12). Mental illnesses or disorders that *may* affect capacity include bipolar disorder or manic depression, major depression, and schizophrenia.

- "Mental retardation" or developmental disability is defined as "significantly subaverage general intellectual functioning, existing concurrently with deficits in adaptive behavior and manifested before age 22." G.S. 35A-1101(13).

- "Inebriety" is defined as "the habitual use of alcohol or drugs rendering a person incompetent to transact ordinary business concerning the person's estate, dangerous to person or property, cruel and intolerable to family, or unable to provide for family." G.S. 35A-1101(11).

- "Autism" is defined as "a physical disorder of the brain which causes disturbances in the developmental rate of physical, social, and language skills; abnormal responses to sensations; absence of or delay in speech or language; or abnormal ways of relating to people, objects, and events." G.S. 35A-1101(1).

- "Cerebral palsy" is defined as "a muscle dysfunction, characterized by impairment of movement, often combined with speech impairment, and caused by abnormality of or damage to the brain." G.S. 35A-1101(2).

- "Epilepsy" is defined as a neurological condition characterized by abnormal electrical-chemical discharges in the brain manifested in seizures or other physical activities that range from momentary lapses of consciousness to convulsive movements. G.S. 35A-1101(5).

It is important to note that the statutory definitions of mental illness, mental retardation (developmental disability), inebriety, autism, cerebral palsy, and epilepsy either differ from the definitions of mental disorders contained in, or are not defined in, the *Diagnostic and Statistical Manual of Mental Disorders-IV* (DSM-IV).

It is also important to note that the statutory definitions of mental illness and inebriety focus on the cognitive or functional impairments resulting from an individual's mental illness or inebriety and not solely on the person's mental or physical condition. This is also true with respect to some, though not all, of the diagnoses of mental disorders contained in the *Diagnostic and Statistical Manual of Mental Disorders-IV* (DSM-IV).

Senility. G.S. 35A-1101 does not define "senility." The term "senility" is outdated, imprecise, and inaccurate, and generally has been replaced by the term "dementia." "Dementia" has many different causes and is characterized by a decline in memory in association with a decline in other cognitive abilities, such as judgment or abstract thinking, or changes in personality. Dementia occurs disproportionately among senior citizens. "Old age," however, is not a sufficient basis, standing alone, to find a respondent incapacitated. *See Goodson v. Lehmon*, 224 N.C. 616 (1944).

Other mental or physical conditions. Although the medical component of North Carolina's definition of incapacity includes any "disease, injury, or . . . condition" similar to the particular mental and physical disorders listed in G.S. 35A-1101(7), these "other" diseases, injuries, or conditions must be such that they are proximately related to the respondent's inability to make or communicate important decisions regarding his or her person, family, or property or to manage his or her own affairs and property. Other diseases, injuries, or conditions that *may* affect capacity include alcoholic dementia, Alzheimer's disease, coma or persistent vegetative state, delirium, frontal or frototemporal dementia, Jacob-Creutzfeldt disease, diffuse Lewy body dementia, Parkinson's disease, stroke or cerebral vascular accident, traumatic brain injury, vascular dementia, and dementia resulting from AIDS, Huntington's disease, or amyotrophic lateral sclerosis (Lou Gehrig's disease).

D. Incapacity and Physical Impairments

Physical disorders, disease, and conditions that result in physical impairments or limit an individual's physical ability to care for himself or herself or perform normal activities of daily living are *not* sufficient to prove that a respondent is incapacitated unless they also result in the respondent's inability to make or communicate important decisions regarding his or her person, family, or property or significantly limit the respondent's *mental or cognitive capacity* to manage his or her own affairs or property. *See Goodson v. Lehmon*, 224 N.C. 616 (1944); *Cox v. Jefferson-Pilot Fire & Casualty Co.*, 80 N.C. App. 122 (1986). For example, the noted English physicist, Stephen Hawking, suffers from amyotrophic lateral sclerosis (Lou Gehrig's disease), is unable to walk, is unable to speak (except through the use of a keypad and voice synthesizer), has almost no use of his extremities, and cannot feed, dress, toilet, or bathe himself. There is no question that he is physically disabled and functionally impaired with respect to most activities of daily living and instrumental activities of daily living. But it is equally clear that, so far, his medical condition has not limited his general mental or cognitive capacity, has not significantly limited his mental or cognitive capacity to manage his own affairs and property or to make important decisions regarding his person, family, or property, and has not resulted in his being unable to communicate his decisions to others.

E. Proof of Medical Condition

The medical component of incapacity generally must be proved by the testimony of a medical expert who has examined the respondent or the respondent's medical records or other information regarding the respondent's condition, or by information from the respondent's medical records indicating that the respondent has been diagnosed as suffering from mental illness or another mental or physical disorder, disease, or condition.

Proof that a respondent is mentally ill, is developmentally disabled (mentally retarded), is an inebriate, an alcoholic or drug addict or substance abuser, is autistic, suffers from cerebral palsy or epilepsy, is senile or suffers from dementia, or has any other mental or physical disorder, disease, or condition, is not sufficient, in and of itself, to prove that the respondent is incapacitated.

6.6
The Functional and Cognitive Elements of Incapacity

A. Statutory Definition

The functional and cognitive elements of incapacity refer to

- the respondent's mental or cognitive ability to manage his or her own affairs and property, and

- the respondent's mental, cognitive, or physical ability to make or communicate important decisions regarding his or her person, family, or property.

Although functional and cognitive elements of incapacity could be viewed as two separate and distinct "tests" of incapacity, the "division between the functional . . . [and cognitive aspects of incapacity] is somewhat artificial, since functional capacity depends in part on . . . [mental or cognitive] capacity." *See* Stephen J. Anderer, *Determining Competency in Guardianship Proceedings* (Washington, DC: American Bar Association, 1990), 27. The truth, therefore, is that the functional and cognitive aspects of incapacity are more accurately viewed as two related and complementary elements of incapacity, both of which focus primarily on a respondent's ability to perform particular functions—managing his or her own affairs and making important decisions regarding his or her person, family, or property—that require some degree of mental or cognitive capacity.

B. Nature and Purpose

The functional or cognitive element of incapacity is much more important than the medical component of incapacity. A respondent's functional or cognitive impairment, therefore, should be the primary focus of a proceeding to appoint a guardian for an allegedly incapacitated adult. Nonetheless, proof that a respondent is cognitively or functionally impaired is insufficient to establish a respondent's incapacity without evidence that the respondent's incapacity results from an identified mental or physical impairment, disease, injury, or condition.

It is important to note, again, that the standard for determining whether a respondent is incapacitated focuses on whether the respondent lacks *sufficient* capacity to manage his or her own affairs or property or to make or communicate important decisions regarding his or her person, family, or property. The issue, therefore, is not whether the respondent's mental or cognitive capacity is optimal or unimpaired, but rather whether his or her mental or cognitive capacity is *minimally adequate* to enable him or her to function, make decisions, and care for his or her personal needs and financial affairs at the level that is necessary to ensure his or her own well-being, protection, and safety. Nor is it sufficient to prove that another person might manage a respondent's affairs or property more wisely or efficiently than the respondent. *See Hagins v. Greensboro Redevelopment Comm'n*, 275 N.C. 90 (1969).

And, finally, because the functional and cognitive elements of incapacity focus primarily on the respondent's *mental or cognitive* capacity or incapacity, it is important to note that a respondent's *physical* capacity or incapacity is irrelevant in determining the respondent's incapacity *unless* it significantly affects his or her ability to make or communicate important decisions regarding his or her person, family, or property. *See Goodson v. Lehmon*, 224 N.C. 616 (1944). For this reason, proof that a respondent is unable, due to a physical impairment, disease, injury, or condition, to perform some or all of the activities of daily living (ADLs)—or even some or all of the instrumental activities of daily living (IADLs)—is insufficient to prove that the respondent is incapacitated.

C. Capacity to Manage One's Affairs

The first prong of the functional element of incapacity (which dates back at least to 1883) focuses on the respondent's capacity to manage his or her own affairs. It is, nominally at least, an objective standard that focuses on the respondent's actual and potential functioning—the respondent's behavior and actions with respect to his or her person, family, and property. It focuses more on the *outcome* of the respondent's decisions than on the respondent's decisions themselves or the *process* by which the respondent makes decisions.

The functional element of incapacity theoretically distinguishes "clinical incapacity" from "legal incapacity." *See* Charles P. Sabatino and Suzanna L. Basinger, *Competency: Reforming Our Legal Fictions*, 6 J. MENTAL HEALTH & AGING 119 (2000). Requiring proof that a respondent is functionally impaired in the sense of being unable to adequately manage his or her affairs or property is intended to ensure that the State intervenes only when necessary to protect a substantial personal or property interest of the respondent that is threatened due to the respondent's condition. *See* Stephen J. Anderer, *Determining Competency in Guardianship*

Proceedings (Washington, DC: American Bar Association, 1990), 10. The functional element of incapacity also may implicitly incorporate the element of "necessity" by requiring objective proof that a respondent's property, health, safety, or welfare will be harmed as a result of his or her impairment.

Functional definitions of incapacity, however, are often vague and imprecise and, too often, are applied subjectively by concluding that a respondent who behaves or acts in an "unreasonable" or "irrational" manner must be mentally incompetent.

G.S. 35A-1101 does not define the phrase "lacks sufficient capacity to manage . . . [his or her] own affairs." Nor is there an abundance of case law that interprets this aspect of the statutory definition of incapacity.

A 1969 decision by the North Carolina Supreme Court, however, suggests that a person lacks sufficient capacity to manage his or her own affairs if his or her mental or cognitive impairment is such that he or she is incapable of

- transacting the ordinary business involved in taking care of his or her property, health, or personal safety or welfare,

- exercising rational judgment, and

- weighing the consequences of his or her acts upon himself or herself, his or her family, or his or her property and estate.

See Hagins v. Greensboro Redevelopment Comm'n, 275 N.C. 90 (1969).

Conversely, a person does not lack sufficient capacity to manage his or her own affairs if he or she

- understands what is necessarily required for the management of his or her ordinary personal and business affairs,

- is able to perform those acts with reasonable continuity,

- comprehends the effect of what he or she does, and

- can exercise his or her own will.

See Hagins v. Greensboro Redevelopment Comm'n, 275 N.C. 90 (1969). *See also Cox v. Jefferson-Pilot Fire & Casualty Co.*, 80 N.C. App. 122 (1986); *Soderlund v. N.C. School of the Arts*, 125 N.C. App. 386 (1997); *State Farm Fire & Casualty Co. v. Darsie*, 161 N.C. App. 542 (2003).

A person's "affairs" encompass all of an individual's personal, business, and financial affairs. *See Hagins v. Greensboro Redevelopment Comm'n*, 275 N.C. 90 (1969). More specifically, a person's "affairs" include matters relating to his or her

- health care,

- personal safety,

- residence,

- nutrition,

- clothing,

- personal hygiene,

- family relationships,

- personal relationships,

- finances,

- business, and

- property.

D.   Capacity to Make and Communicate Important Decisions

The second prong of the functional or cognitive element of incapacity, which was first added to North Carolina's guardianship statute in 1977 and was made generally applicable in all adult guardianship proceedings in 1987, focuses directly on deficiencies in a respondent's cognitive functioning by examining the respondent's mental or cognitive capacity to make or communicate important decisions regarding his or her person, family, or property.

The cognitive element of incapacity focuses directly on deficiencies in a respondent's cognitive functioning. In theory, the cognitive element of incapacity provides an objective standard that allows individuals who have at least a minimally adequate level of mental and cognitive capacity to make "unreasonable," "irrational," "unwise," "ill-advised," "foolish," "stupid," or even self-destructive decisions as long as they do so through the use of a "rational" decision-making process.

It is important to note that the cognitive element of incapacity focuses on an individual's decision-making *capacity*, rather than the behaviors or actions that may result from the individual's decisions or inability to make a decision. Stated differently, this "test" of incapacity focuses on the respondent's ability to make "rational" decisions or the *process* through which the respondent makes decisions, rather than the *content* of the respondent's decisions or the behaviors, actions, or consequences that result from the respondent's decisions or inability to make "rational" decisions. The issue, therefore, is not whether a respondent's decisions appear, to a reasonable or rational observer, to be unreasonable, irrational, unwise, ill-advised, stupid, or even self-destructive, but rather whether some mental or physical impairment renders the respondent incapable of making rational decisions or significantly limits the respondent's ability to do so.

At a minimum, assessments of a respondent's cognitive functioning should focus on the respondent's

- awareness,

- perception,

- orientation to reality,

- concentration,

- memory,

- comprehension,
- insight,
- reasoning,
- deliberation,
- appreciation of consequences, and
- choice.

A respondent may lack sufficient capacity to make important decisions concerning his or her person, family, or property if he or she

- cannot understand or appreciate the facts that are relevant in connection with a particular decision or situation;
- is unable to express a choice or preference with respect to a particular decision or situation;
- is unable to understand the risks, benefits, and alternatives with respect to a particular decision or situation;
- is unable to appreciate the consequences of a particular decision or situation; or
- is unable to weigh, in a rational manner and consistent with his or her values, the relative risks, benefits, and consequences involved in a particular decision or situation.

Although G.S. 35A-1101 does not define the phrase "important decisions concerning . . . [the respondent's] person, family, or property," it clearly includes decisions regarding the respondent's health, safety, welfare, personal and family affairs, and business and financial affairs.

6.7
Clinical Assessment of Cognitive and Functional Incapacity

Medical or clinical assessments of capacity or incapacity are different from legal determinations of capacity or incapacity. Clinical assessments of an individual's mental, cognitive, or functional capacity, however, are relevant in determining whether, in the context of a legal proceeding to appoint a guardian for that individual, he or she is "incompetent" or incapacitated.

A. General Mental Capacity

Clinical evaluations of an individual's *general* mental capacity or incapacity assess the extent to which the individual's cognitive functioning is *minimally adequate* in the areas of

- word knowledge,
- recent and remote memory,
- perceptual accuracy or reality testing,
- insight,

- abstraction, and

- executive functioning and judgment in both the personal and social spheres.

B. Specific Cognitive and Functional Capacity

In most cases, a clinical evaluation of an individual's capacity or incapacity also should focus more particularly on an individual's specific capacity with respect to one or more cognitive or functional "domains" (areas of cognitive or functional behavior), such as consenting to medical treatment, engaging in financial transactions, or caring for oneself in an independent living situation.

C. Clinical Evaluation of Incapacity

Clinical evaluations of an individual's capacity or incapacity should be based on a thorough professional assessment of the individual's

- cognitive capacity,

- medical or mental diagnosis and condition,

- functional capacity, and

- environment, context, and situation.

Cognitive capacity. An individual's cognitive capacity refers to his or her general mental capacity or ability in the areas of attention, concentration, perception, memory, understanding, comprehension, deliberation, reasoning, and judgment. Clinicians assess an individual's cognitive capacity through clinical interviews and cognitive testing. *See* Appendix 6-8, Cognition and Cognitive Testing and Appendix 6-9, Brief Guide to Psychological and Neuropsychological Instruments. Some instruments, such as the Folstein Mini Mental Status Examination (MMSE), which is a short test that assesses an individual's awareness of time, place, and orientation, comprehension and production of language, short-term memory, and ability to attend and concentrate, may be used as an initial screening device to determine whether an individual *may* be cognitively impaired but are not determinative with respect to whether an individual is or isn't cognitively impaired.

Medical diagnosis. An accurate medical diagnosis of an individual's mental and physical condition is important in determining whether the individual is cognitively impaired, the cause of the individual's impairment, the likely extent of the individual's impairment, whether the individual's impairment is permanent or temporary, whether the individual's condition will improve or get worse, whether treatment may improve the individual's condition, and what treatment might help improve the individual's condition. Cognitive impairments may be caused by cognitive disorders such as dementia, by psychiatric disorders such as schizophrenia, by other medical conditions, such as stroke or traumatic brain injury, or by other factors such as substance abuse. Diagnoses of mental impairments are listed and described in the *Diagnostic and Statistical Manual of Mental Disorders-IV* (DSM-IV). *See also* Appendix 6-2, Medical Conditions Affecting Capacity; Appendix 6-3, Dementia Overview; Appendix 6-4, Temporary and Reversible Causes of Confusion; Appendix 6-5, Medications That May Commonly Cause Confusion; and Appendix 6-6, Distinguishing Delirium from

Dementia. A diagnosis that an individual suffers from a mental illness, developmental disability, or other medical condition, however, is not, in and of itself, sufficient to support a conclusion that the individual lacks mental capacity.

Functional capacity. An individual's functional capacity refers to the mental capacity required to perform particular functions or activities, such as making decisions regarding medical treatment, financial transactions, or personal care. For example, mental capacity to consent to or refuse medical treatment generally is understood to require

- the capacity or ability to understand or comprehend information regarding one's medical diagnosis and the potential risks and benefits of medical treatments;

- the ability to appreciate the significance or applicability of that information to one's own situation;

- the ability to make a reasoned choice by rationally evaluating the benefits and risks of medical treatment in light of one's own life and values; and

- the ability to communicate a definite and consistent decision regarding medical treatment.

Similarly, assessments of functional capacity in the domain of financial matters examine an individual's knowledge (ability to describe facts, concepts, and events related to financial activities); skills (the ability to make change, write checks, or perform other activities related to financial activities); and judgment (the ability to make rational or reasonably sound financial decisions). The concepts of functional and cognitive impairment are related to the extent that an individual's cognitive impairment may impair his or her ability to perform certain functions. Functional capacity, however, must be assessed separately from an individual's general cognitive capacity because the fact that an individual has a cognitive impairment does not necessarily mean that his or her cognitive impairment limits his or her ability to perform a particular function. Clinicians assess functional capacity through direct observation, reports from family members, performance-based testing, and functional instruments. *See* Appendix 6-10, Everyday Functioning and Functional Assessment; Appendix 6-11, Activities of Daily Living; and Appendix 6-12, Instrumental Activities of Daily Living. A respondent's ability to perform instrumental activities of daily living (IADLs) *may* be relevant to the issue of the respondent's mental or cognitive capacity. Assessments of a respondent's ability to perform normal activities of daily living (ADLs) generally are not relevant to the issue of the respondent's mental or cognitive capacity, but may be useful in determining the needs of an incapacitated ward or developing a guardianship plan for an incapacitated ward.

Environmental assessment. Assessment of an individual's environment, context, and situation examines the degree to which an individual's personal, social, and physical environments affect his or her capacity, the personal, physical, psychosocial, and situational demands that are placed on the individual, the individual's personal history, values, and preferences, the personal, social, and other resources that are available to the individual, and the situational risks to the individual. Clinicians assess an individual's environment, context, and situation through direct questioning of the individual or through information obtained from the individual's family or other sources.

6.8
Multidisciplinary Evaluations of Incapacity

A. Statutory Definition

A multidisciplinary evaluation (MDE) is a court-ordered evaluation of a respondent's incapacity conducted in connection with an adult guardianship proceeding. *See* G.S. 35A-1101(14).

B. Obtaining an MDE

The procedures for requesting and obtaining an MDE are discussed in detail in Chapter 5 of this manual.

C. Preparing an MDE

A multidisciplinary evaluation must be conducted, prepared, coordinated, or assembled by a state or local social service, public health, mental health, vocational rehabilitation, diagnostic evaluation, or human service agency designated in the Clerk's order directing the evaluation. *See* G.S. 35A-1111(b); G.S. 35A-1101(4). When a state or local human services agency is the petitioner in a pending guardianship proceeding, that agency should not be designated to conduct, prepare, coordinate, or assemble a multidisciplinary evaluation of the respondent. An agency that has been designated to perform a multidisciplinary evaluation may perform the multidisciplinary evaluation itself (if its staff includes a doctor, psychologist, and social worker), request other state or local human services agencies to conduct all or part of the evaluation, or contract with doctors, psychologists, and social workers who are not employed by state or local human services agencies to conduct all or part of the evaluation.

D. Purpose of the MDE

The purposes of a multidisciplinary evaluation are to assist the Clerk in determining whether the respondent is incapacitated, the nature and extent of a respondent's incapacity, and the needs of the respondent that should be addressed in a guardianship plan. *See* G.S. 35A-1111(a).

E. Nature and Scope of the MDE

A multidisciplinary evaluation must contain current medical, psychological, and social work evaluations of the respondent. An evaluation is considered to be "current" if it has been done within the year immediately preceding a guardianship hearing. In ordering a multidisciplinary evaluation, the Clerk may direct that these evaluations address specific issues or questions regarding the respondent's alleged incapacity. The Clerk also may order the respondent to attend a multidisciplinary evaluation for the purpose of being evaluated. G.S. 35A-1111(d).

Medical component. The medical component of a multidisciplinary evaluation should be completed by a licensed physician or other qualified medical professional who has examined the respondent or reviewed the respondent's medical records. The physician who completes the medical component of a multidisciplinary evaluation need not be a psychiatrist. At a minimum, the medical component of a multidisciplinary evaluation should provide current information regarding the respondent's physical and neurological status, relevant medical history, diagnoses of physical and mental disorders, conditions, or impairments, etiology of and prognosis for the respondent's impairments and condition, current and recommended medical treatment (including medications), results of pertinent tests, and clinical impressions of the respondent's medical condition.

Psychological component. The psychological component of a multidisciplinary evaluation should be conducted by a licensed clinical psychologist or other qualified mental health professional (such as a psychiatrist or licensed clinical social worker) who has examined the respondent or reviewed the respondent's medical and mental health records and other relevant information. At a minimum, the psychological component of a multidisciplinary evaluation should provide current information regarding the respondent's mental health, intellectual functioning, emotional status, and adaptive behavior, diagnoses of mental disorders, conditions, or impairments, etiology of and prognosis for the respondent's impairments and condition, current and recommended treatment (including medications), results of pertinent tests, and clinical impressions of the respondent's mental condition.

Social work component. The social work component of a multidisciplinary evaluation should be conducted by a qualified social worker who has examined the respondent or obtained reliable information regarding the respondent's situation. At a minimum, the social work component of a multidisciplinary evaluation should provide current information regarding the personal, family, social, and environmental aspects of the respondent's life, including a description and assessment of the respondent's living situation, family and interpersonal relationships, available family and community support and resources, employment, transportation, performance of activities of daily living, and performance of instrumental activities of daily living, as well as clinical impressions of the respondent's personal, family, and social condition.

Other assessments. Multidisciplinary evaluations also may include current evaluations by professionals in the areas of education, vocational rehabilitation, occupational therapy, vocational therapy, psychiatry, speech and hearing, and communications disorders.

Summary and report of assessment. A multidisciplinary evaluation should include a summary, prepared by the designated agency or one or more of the professionals who evaluated the respondent, that assesses whether the respondent is or may be "incompetent" or incapacitated, and, if so, assesses the nature and extent of the respondent's incapacity. If a respondent has the capacity to make particular decisions or perform certain activities, the summary should indicate the areas in which the respondent retains sufficient capacity to manage his or her affairs and recommend the creation of a limited guardianship. The agency's or professionals' report also may make recommendations with respect to a guardianship plan that will meet the respondent's needs, the ways in which a guardian should assist or care for the respondent, the persons or agencies that are most qualified or suitable to serve as the respondent's guardian or guardians, and the manner in which the respondent's guardianship should be monitored, reviewed, or reassessed.

6.9
Judicial Determination of Incapacity

A. Determination by Clerk, Judge, or Jury

Determinations of mental incapacity or "incompetency" under G.S. Ch. 35A, Art. 1 are made by the Clerk of Superior Court, by a jury if a jury trial has been properly demanded or ordered pursuant to G.S. 35A-1110, or by a Superior Court Judge (or jury) if an order adjudicating a respondent's incapacity is appealed to the Superior Court pursuant to G.S. 35A-1115.

B. Statutory Elements

To find a respondent incapacitated, the Clerk (or jury or judge) must find that

- the respondent lacks sufficient capacity to manage his or her affairs or to make or communicate important decisions regarding his or her person, family, or property, *and*
- the respondent's lack of capacity is due to mental illness, mental retardation, epilepsy, cerebral palsy, autism, inebriety, senility, disease, injury, or similar cause or condition.

C. Determinations of Fact and Law

The issue of incapacity, for purposes of appointing a guardian to manage the personal or financial affairs of an adult, involves a *legal*, rather than a medical or social, determination of the adult's capacity to make decisions and manage his or her personal or financial affairs.

D. Evidence of Incapacity

In determining whether a respondent is incapacitated, the Clerk (or jury or judge) should consider evidence regarding

- the respondent's medical condition;
- the respondent's cognition;
- the respondent's everyday functioning;
- the respondent's values and preferences;
- the risk of harm to the respondent or the respondent's property resulting from the respondent's incapacity and the level of supervision needed to protect the respondent or the respondent's property; and
- the means that may be available to enhance the respondent's capacity.

If the Clerk (or jury or judge) determines that the respondent is not incapacitated, the Clerk (or judge) must enter an order dismissing the proceeding.

E. Standard of Proof

In order to find a respondent incapacitated, the Clerk's (or jury's or judge's) findings must be based on clear, cogent, and convincing evidence. G.S. 35A-1112(d); *In re Efird*, 114 N.C. App. 635 (1994).

F. Finding Regarding Incapacity

An order appointing a guardian for an incapacitated respondent should include findings regarding the nature and extent of the respondent's incapacity. *See* G.S. 35A-1112(d). If the Clerk orders a limited guardianship, the Clerk's order must include findings regarding the nature and extent of the respondent's incapacity as they relate to the respondent's need for a guardian. G.S. 35A-1215(b).

G. The Judicial Decision-Making Process

When the Clerk adjudicates the issue of incapacity and appoints a guardian for an incapacitated respondent, the Clerk's order should

- appropriately balance the respondent's well-being and rights;
- promote the respondent's rights to autonomy and self-determination to the greatest extent possible;
- identify and take advantage of less restrictive alternatives to guardianship whenever possible;
- provide appropriate guidance to guardians and establish procedures for monitoring guardianship; and
- limit the scope of guardianship when a limited guardianship is appropriate.

H. Limited Guardianship Orders

When the Clerk orders a limited guardianship, the Clerk's order should specify the legal rights that will be retained by the ward and the limits that are imposed with respect to the guardian's powers and duties. G.S. 35A-1215(b).

Appendix 6-1
Clinical Professionals

Reprinted by permission of the American Bar Association and the American Psychological Association from *Judicial Determination of Capacity of Older Adults in Guardianship Proceedings*.

Note: The information provided in this appendix is meant to highlight some of the strengths that varied professionals may bring to the capacity evaluation practice. It is not meant to define or limit the absolute, necessary, or full scope of practice for these professionals, but rather to highlight some potential strengths each discipline may bring to the capacity evaluation process.

A clinician is a general term for a healthcare professional who works with patients. A wide range of clinicians may bring expertise to the capacity evaluation process.

Geriatricians, geriatric psychiatrists, or geropsychologists are practitioners with specialized training in aging. They are experienced in considering the multiple medical, social, and psychological factors that may impact an older adult's functioning. A geriatric assessment team is comprised of multiple disciplines, each with advanced training in syndromes of aging.

Neurologists are medical doctors (M.D.) with specialized training in brain function. They may address how specific neurological conditions (e.g., dementia) are affecting the individual and his or her capacity.

Neuropsychologists are psychologists with specialized training in cognitive testing. They may address relationships between neurological conditions, cognitive tests results, and an individual's functional abilities.

Nurses have medical expertise and some, such as visiting nurses in Area Agencies on Aging, may have in-depth information on how a person's medical condition is impacting functioning in the home. Geriatric nurse practitioners are advanced practice nurses with additional credentials to assess and treat the medical problems of aging.

Occupational therapists are professionals with advanced degrees specializing in the assessment of an individual's functioning on everyday tasks, such as eating, meal preparation, bill paying, cleaning, and shopping.

Physicians are medical doctors (M.D.). Physicians who are primary care clinicians or internists can provide a summary of the individual's major medical conditions. In some cases, the physician may have provided care to the individual over many years and can provide a historical perspective on the individual's functioning (although this cannot be assumed).

Psychiatrists are medical doctors (M.D.) with specialized training in mental health. They may address how specific psychiatric conditions (e.g., schizophrenia) and related emotional and mental systems may be affecting the individual and his or her capacity. Geropsychiatrists receive additional training in problems of aging; forensic psychiatrists receive additional training in mental health and the law.

Psychologists are clinicians with advanced training in behavioral health. They may utilize standardized testing and in-depth assessment, which is useful when the judge wants detailed information about areas of cognitive or behavioral strengths or weaknesses. Geropsychologists receive additional training in problems of aging; forensic psychologists receive additional training in mental health and the law.

Social workers are trained to consider the multiple determinants on an individual's social functioning, and are often knowledgeable about a wide range of social and community services that may assist the individual.

Appendix 6-2
Medical Conditions Affecting Capacity

Reprinted by permission of the American Bar Association and the American Psychological Association from *Judicial Determination of Capacity of Older Adults in Guardianship Proceedings*.

Dementia is a general term for a medical condition characterized by a loss of memory and functioning. Primary degenerative dementias are those with disease processes that result in a deteriorating course, including Alzheimer's disease, Lewy Body Dementia, and Frontal Dementia (each associated with a type of abnormal brain cell).

Condition	Source	Symptoms	Treatability
Alcoholic Dementia	A fairly common form of dementia, caused by long-term abuse of alcohol, usually for 20 years or more. Alcohol is a neurotoxin that passes the blood-brain barrier.	Memory loss, problem solving difficulty, and impairments in visuospatial function are commonly found in patients with alcohol dementia.	Alcohol dementia is partially reversible, if there is long term sobriety—cessation of use. There is evidence to suggest that some damaged brain tissue may regenerate following extended sobriety, leading to modest improvements in thinking and function.
Alzheimer's disease ("AD")	Most common type of dementia, caused by a progressive brain disease involving protein deposits in brain and disruption of neurotransmitter systems.	Initial short-term memory loss, followed by problems in language and communication, orientation to time and place, everyday problem solving, and eventually recognition of people and everyday objects. In the early stages, an individual may retain some decisional and functional abilities.	Progressive and irreversible, resulting ultimately in a terminal state. Medications may improve symptoms and cause a temporary brightening of function in the earlier stages.
Bipolar Disorder or Manic Depression	A psychiatric illness characterized by alternating periods of mania and depression.	Affects functional and decisional abilities in the manic stage or when the depressed stage is severe.	Can be treated with medications, but requires a strong commitment to treatment on the part of the individual. Varies over time; periodic re-evaluation is needed.

Condition	Source	Symptoms	Treatability
Coma	A state of temporary or permanent unconsciousness.	Minimally responsive or unresponsive, unable to communicate decisions and needs a substitute decision maker.	Often temporary; regular re-evaluation required.
Delirium	A temporary confusional state with a wide variety of causes, such as dehydration, poor nutrition, multiple medication use, medication reaction, anesthesia, metabolic imbalances, and infections.	Substantially impaired attention and significant decisional and functional impairments across many domains. May be difficult to distinguish from the confusion and inattention characteristic of dementia.	Often temporary and reversible. If untreated may proceed to a dementia. It is important to rule out delirium before diagnosing dementia. To do so, a good understanding of the history and course of functional decline, as well as a full medical work-up, are necessary.
Frontal or Frontotemporal Dementia (Pick's disease is one example)	Broad category of dementia caused by brain diseases or small strokes that affect the frontal lobes of the brain.	Problems with personality and behavior are often the first changes, followed by problems in organization, judgment, insight, motivation, and the ability to engage in goal-oriented behavior.	Early in their disease, patients may have areas of retained functional ability, but as disease progresses they can rapidly lose all decisional capacity.
Jacob-Creutzfeldt Disease	A rare type of progressive dementia affecting humans that is related to 'mad cow' disease.	The disease usually has a rapid course, with death occurring within two years of initial symptoms. These include fatigue, mental slowing, depression, bizarre ideations, confusion, and motor disturbances, including muscular jerking, leading finally to a vegetative state and death.	There is no treatment currently and the disease is relentlessly progressive.

Condition	Source	Symptoms	Treatability
Diffuse Lewy Body Dementia (DLB)	A type of dementia on the Parkinson disease spectrum.	DLB involves mental changes that precede or co-occur with motor changes. Visual hallucinations are common, as are fluctuations in mental capacity.	This disease is progressive and there are no known treatments. Parkinson medications are often of limited use.
Major Depression	A very common psychiatric illness.	Sad or disinterested mood, poor appetite, energy, sleep, and concentration, feelings of hopelessness, helplessness, and suicidality. In severe cases, very poor hygiene, hallucinations, delusions, and impaired decisional and functional abilities.	Treatable and reversible, although in some resistant cases electroconvulsive therapy (ECT) is needed.
Developmental Disorders ("DD") including Mental Retardation ("MR")	Brain-related conditions that begin at birth or childhood (before age 18) and continue throughout adult life. MR concerns low-level intellectual functioning with functional deficits that can be found across many kinds of DD, including autism, Down syndrome, and cerebral palsy.	Functioning tends to be stable over time but lower than normal peers. MR is most commonly mild. Some conditions such as Downs syndrome may develop a supervening dementia later in life, causing decline in already limited decisional and functional abilities.	Not reversible, but everyday functioning can be improved with a wide range of supports, interventions, and less restrictive alternatives. Individuals with DD have a wide range of decisional and functional abilities and, thus, require careful assessment by skilled clinicians.
Parkinson's Disease (PD)	Progressive brain disease that initially affects motor function, but in many cases proceeds to dementia.	PD presents initially with problems with tremors and physical movement, followed by problems with expression and thinking, and leading sometimes to dementia after a number of years.	PD is progressive, but motor symptoms can be treated for many years. Eventually, medications become ineffective and most physical and mental capacities are lost. Evaluation of capacity must avoid confusion of physical for cognitive impairment.

Condition	Source	Symptoms	Treatability
Persistent Vegetative State (PSV)	A state of minimal or no responsiveness following emergence from coma.	Patient is mute and immobile with an absence of all higher mental activity. Cannot communicate decisions and requires a substitute decision maker for all areas.	Cases of PSV usually lead to death within a year's time.
Schizophrenia	A chronic brain-based psychiatric illness	Hallucinations and delusions; poor judgment, insight, planning, personal hygiene, and interpersonal skills. May range from mild to severe, and impact on functional and decisional abilities, are likewise variable.	Many symptoms can be successfully treated with medication. Capacity loss often occurs when patients go off their medications.
Stroke or Cerebral Vascular Accident ("CVA")	A significant bleeding in the brain, or a blockage of oxygen to the brain.	May affect just one part of the brain, so individuals should be carefully assessed to determine their functional and decisional abilities.	Some level of recovery and improved function over the first year; thus a temporary guardianship might be considered if the stroke is recent.
Traumatic Brain Injury ("TBI")	A blow to the head that usually involves loss of consciousness.	Individuals with mild and moderate TBI may appear superficially the same as before the accident, but have persisting problems with motivation, judgment, and organization. Those with severe TBI may have profound problems with everyday functioning.	Usually show recovery of thinking and functional abilities over the first year; thus a temporary guardianship should be considered if the injury is recent.
Vascular Dementia ("VaD")	Multiple strokes that accumulate and cause dementia.	Decisional and functional strengths and weaknesses may vary, depending on the extent and location of the strokes.	May remain stable over time if underlying cerebrovascular or heart disease is successfully managed.

Appendix 6-3
Dementia Overview

Reprinted by permission of the American Bar Association and the American Psychological Association from *Assessment of Older Adults with Diminished Capacity*.[1]

What is dementia?

Dementia is a syndrome characterized by decline in memory in association with either decline in other cognitive abilities, e.g., judgment and abstract thinking, or personality change. The resulting impairment must be severe enough to interfere with work or usual social activities or relationships. The requirement for decline distinguishes dementia from life-long mental retardation, although a person with mental retardation can develop dementia if his or her cognitive abilities decline from a previous level. The requirement also means that a person with high previous intelligence can have dementia if his or her cognitive abilities decline to average levels, and this decline interferes with work or usual social activities or relationships. Outdated terms: terms that were used in the past, such as *senility*, *chronic brain syndrome*, and *hardening of the arteries*, are rarely used now because they are imprecise and inaccurate.

What causes dementia?

Dementia can be caused by more than 70 diseases and conditions. The most common cause is Alzheimer's disease, which is present in 60 percent to 75 percent of dementia cases in the United States. The second most common cause is vascular or multi-infarct disease, which is present in 10 percent to 20 percent of cases.

Alzheimer's disease and multi-infarct disease often coexist in a condition referred to as *mixed dementia*. Other diseases and conditions that can cause dementia include Lewy body disease, fronto-temporal disease (including Pick's disease), Creutzfeld-Jacob disease, Parkinson's disease, Huntington's disease, amyotrophic lateral sclerosis (Lou Gehrig's disease), and AIDS.

Reversible dementia. In a small minority of people with dementia, the condition may be partially or completely reversible with treatment of underlying causes, such as chronic infections, thyroid disease, and normal pressure hydrocephalus. Unfortunately, these situations are rare.

How common is dementia?

The total number of people with dementia in the United States is not known. That is because most people with dementia do not have a diagnosis, and no study with a nationally representative sample and procedures for diagnosing dementia has been completed.

---

1. Prepared by Katie Maslow, M.S.W., of the Alzheimer's Association, Washington, D.C. [references omitted]. *Assessment of Older Adults with Diminished Capacity* is available on-line at: www.apa.org/pi/aging/diminished_capacity.pdf.

Estimates of the number of people with Alzheimer's disease come from studies of smaller community samples. Results of two widely cited studies indicate that 2 percent of people age 65 to 74 have Alzheimer's disease, with the proportion increasing to 8 percent to 19 percent of people age 75 to 84, and 29 percent to 42 percent of people age 85 and over. Combining these proportions and U.S. Census data indicates that 2.6 million to 4.5 million people age 65 and over (7 percent to 13 percent of all people age 65 and over) had Alzheimer's disease in 2000. Since prevalence rises rapidly with age, the total number of people with Alzheimer's disease will increase greatly as the age groups 75 to 84 and 85+ grow in coming decades. Alzheimer's disease occurs in a small proportion (probably less than one percent) of people under age 65. That proportion may increase in the future as the disease is recognized earlier. Assuming that Alzheimer's disease is present in 60 percent to 75 percent of all cases of dementia in the U.S. and that it affected 2.6 to 4.5 million people age 65 and over in 2000, one could estimate that 3.4 to 7.5 million people age 65 and over had dementia in 2000. Preliminary data from the Health and Retirement Survey indicate that there may be 400,000 people under age 65 with dementia, for a total of 3.9 to 8 million people with dementia in all age groups in 2000.

What are the symptoms of dementia?

As noted above, dementia is characterized by decline in memory associated with decline in other cognitive abilities or personality change. Many descriptions of the symptoms of dementia focus primarily on symptoms of Alzheimer's disease. Symptoms of other dementing diseases and conditions are often described only as they differ from the symptoms of Alzheimer's disease.

Alzheimer's disease generally begins gradually. Its causes are not known, but much has been learned in recent years about the risk factors, biology, and course of the disease.

The earliest symptoms of Alzheimer's disease are usually memory problems, especially problems with learning and recall of new information. Other early symptoms include difficulty with language (e.g., word-finding) and disturbances in visuospatial skills that can result in getting lost in a familiar setting. Deficits in executive functions (e.g., planning, organization, and judgment) are also common. These cognitive changes limit the person's ability to work and carry out activities that are needed for independent living, e.g., driving, shopping, cooking, and managing finances. The person may or may not be aware of, and be disturbed by, these changes. Alzheimer's disease is progressive.

Over time, the person's cognitive deficits worsen, and other kinds of symptoms appear. Many people with Alzheimer's disease are depressed. Some become withdrawn, apathetic, and/or irritable. Agitation is common, and some people with Alzheimer's disease develop psychiatric and behavioral symptoms, e.g., delusions, aggression, wandering, and inappropriate sexual behaviors. Most people with the disease require 24-hour supervision at least in the middle stage of their illness. Eventually, they become unable to bathe, dress, toilet, and feed themselves. Gait and swallowing difficulties are also common in the late stage of the disease. Death usually occurs sooner than would be predicted on the basis of population data.

Vascular or multi-infarct dementia differs from Alzheimer's dementia in that it generally begins more abruptly and exhibits a step-wise progression of symptoms. This is because the condition is usually caused by a stroke, multiple small strokes, or changes in blood supply to the brain that result in specific brain lesions. A person's cognitive and other symptoms depend on the type, location, and extent of these lesions; thus, symptoms vary greatly from one person to another.

Lewy body disease differs from Alzheimer's disease in that it usually progresses more rapidly. Visual hallucinations, fluctuating cognitive abilities, changing attention and alertness, and motor signs of parkinsonism are also more common.

Fronto-temporal disease (including Pick's disease) differs from Alzheimer's disease in that learning ability and visuospatial skills are often less affected, and noncognitive symptoms are more common. Patients frequently exhibit profound apathy, distractability, and impulsivity.

Can stages of dementia be identified?

Various staging systems have been developed for dementia. These systems are useful because they provide a conceptual framework that often helps families, care providers, and others understand where their relative or client is in the course of his or her illness and, therefore, think about and plan for the person's current and future care. Some relatively simple staging systems identify only 3 stages (mild, moderate, and severe) and define the stages in very general terms. Other staging systems are more complex and precise. An example of the latter type is the Global Deterioration Scale, a 7-stage system based on the severity of a person's cognitive and self-care deficits and psychiatric and behavioral symptoms.

Despite the usefulness of this and other staging systems, it is important to remember that the progression of dementing diseases and conditions and the timing of particular symptoms vary greatly from one person to another. Thus few patients progress through the stages exactly as they are defined in any system.

How can cognitive changes that are common in normal aging be distinguished from dementia?

It is often very difficult to distinguish memory problems and other cognitive changes that are common in normal aging from the early symptoms of dementia, in part because cognitive changes in normal aging are not well understood.

In its dementia guideline, the American Medical Association points out that a person with dementia will eventually become unable to maintain independent functioning, whereas independent functioning is preserved in normal aging. To distinguish dementia and normal aging without waiting to see whether the person's functioning worsens, the guideline suggests several comparisons: for example, in dementia, the person's family is likely to be more concerned about his or her forgetfulness, whereas in normal aging, the person may be more concerned; similarly, in dementia, there is likely to be notable decline in memory for recent events and ability to converse, whereas in normal aging, the person remembers important events and maintains the ability to converse. These and other comparisons are helpful but not definitive in distinguishing the two conditions.

Mild Cognitive Impairment is a condition that is receiving increasing attention as researchers attempt to understand the causes of Alzheimer's disease and find ways to prevent and treat it. For research purposes, it is efficient to study people who are at high risk for the disease, and many elderly people are now enrolled as subjects in observational studies and clinical trials where they are diagnosed as having mild cognitive impairment. An unknown number of elderly people are also being diagnosed with mild cognitive impairment outside of research settings. Many researchers and clinicians believe that all people with mild cognitive impairment will eventually transition to Alzheimer's disease. Reported rates of transition range from 6 percent to 25 percent per year in individuals age 66 to 81 at the start of the study. Some clinicians and advocates question the wisdom of diagnosing mild cognitive impairment in people who are quite old at time of diagnosis, may be upset by the diagnosis, may not transition for four or more years, and may be denied insurance and/or admission to certain residential care facilities if the diagnosis is known.

Why is it important to diagnose dementia and the underlying cause of the dementia?

Some physicians are reluctant to diagnose dementia or its underlying cause because they think the conditions are hopeless and are hesitant to call attention to them unless asked by the family. Over the past decade, dementia and its causes are being diagnosed more often, primarily because of the availability of medications for Alzheimer's disease and greater general awareness of Alzheimer's and dementia. Still many people with dementia have not been diagnosed. Physicians may be aware of a patient's cognitive deficits even if they have not conducted a formal evaluation, but even when a formal diagnosis is made, the patient and family may not be told, and the diagnosis may not be entered into his or her medical record.

Diagnosis of dementia is important because it allows the person, and perhaps more so his or her family, to understand what is happening to the person and increases the likelihood that they will access available information and supportive services. It also increases the likelihood that physicians will initiate treatments and be alert to limitations in the person's ability to report symptoms accurately, manage medications safely, and understand and comply with other recommendations. Early diagnosis is important because it gives the person and family time to make financial, legal, and medical decisions while the person is capable.

How can dementia be diagnosed?

Dementia and Alzheimer's disease can be diagnosed with high accuracy (90 percent or higher) when standardized diagnostic criteria are used. Diagnosis of vascular or multi-infarct disease, Lewy body disease, and fronto-temporal disease is often more difficult because many people with these conditions have atypical or nonspecific symptoms.

The first steps in diagnosis are a focused history and physical, mental status testing, and discussions with the family, if any. Laboratory tests are often used, primarily to rule out reversible or partially reversible causes of dementia. There is disagreement about the value of neuroimaging procedures, but virtually all experts agree that these procedures are useful for younger patients and patients with unusual symptoms.

Delirium and depression can present with symptoms similar to dementia. Recognition and differential diagnosis of these three conditions is important. Delirium is an acute condition that can and should be treated quickly. Depression is also treatable in older people. In addition, however, people with dementia are at increased risk of developing delirium, and many people with dementia also have depression; thus, the three conditions often coexist. Effective treatment of coexisting delirium and/or depression may improve cognitive functioning in a person with dementia, although research suggests that treatment for depression often does not have as much effect as expected on the person's cognitive functioning.

Treatment of dementia

Many medical associations and other groups have developed guidelines and consensus statements about treatment of dementia. These documents differ in length, primary focus, and intended audience, but their recommendations are similar. While acknowledging that the effects of available medications for Alzheimer's disease are often modest, the documents generally recommend an initial trial of the medications.

Aggressive treatment of cardiovascular conditions is recommended since these conditions can cause vascular dementia and hasten onset of symptom development in people with Alzheimer's disease. The guidelines and consensus statements recommend careful evaluation of mood and behavioral symptoms and efforts to manage these symptoms nonpharmacologically, if possible. They also recommend treatment of depression, attention to safety issues (e.g., driving, wandering, and firearms), referrals to community services, and involvement and support of family caregivers.

Coexisting medical conditions in people with dementia

Many people with dementia also have other serious medical conditions. Medicare fee-for-service claims for 1999 show, for example, that 30 percent of beneficiaries with dementia also had coronary heart disease, 28 percent also had congestive heart failure, 21 percent also had diabetes, and 16 percent also had thyroid disease. These medical conditions and the medications and other procedures that are used to treat the conditions can worsen cognitive and other symptoms in a person with dementia. At the same time, dementia clearly complicates the treatment of the other conditions. Families and other informal and paid caregivers of people with dementia and co-existing medical conditions are often coping with extremely difficult care situations.

Where do people with dementia live?

No precise information is available about where people with dementia live, but available data suggest that at any one time, about 20 percent of all people with dementia are in nursing homes; about 10 percent are in assisted living or other residential care facilities; and the remaining 70 percent are at home alone or with a family member or other informal caregiver.

People with dementia who live alone. Studies indicate that about 20 percent of people with dementia live alone. About half of these people have a relative or friend who functions as a caregiver, but the other half have no one. Some of these individuals have mild dementia, but many have moderate to severe dementia. They may come to the attention of attorneys when a landlord, neighbor, or law enforcement official realizes they are unable to care for themselves and may create safety problems for others. Lack of an available surrogate decisionmaker may make them difficult clients.

Appendix 6-4
Temporary and Reversible Causes of Confusion

Reprinted by permission of the American Bar Association and the American Psychological Association from *Judicial Determination of Capacity of Older Adults in Guardianship Proceedings*.

Causes of Delirium

If any of these are present:

- Provide appropriate treatment or accommodations.

- Re-assess capacity after treatment or accommodation.

Common Medical Causes Did the evaluator consider how long the problem has been going on? Were standard lab tests and vitals done?	
Drugs	More than 6 meds or more than 3 new meds or use of drugs that cause confusion?
Electrolytes	Low sodium, blood sugar, calcium, etc?
Lack of Drugs, Water, Food	Pain, malnutrition, dehydration?
Infection or Intoxification	Sepsis, urinary track infection, pneumonia; alcohol, metals, solvents?
Reduced Sensory Input	Impaired vision, hearing, nerve conduction?
Intracranial Causes	Subdural hematoma, meningitis, seizure, brain tumor?
Urinary Retention or Fecal Impaction	Drugs, constipation?
Myocardial	Heart attack, heart failure, arrhythmia?
Other Causes of Confusion: Liver or kidney disease Vitamin deficiency Post surgical state	Hepatitis, diabetes, renal failure? Folate, nicotinic acid, thiamine, vitamin B12? Anesthesia, pain?

The Delirium mnemonic is adapted from a chapter by JL Rudolph and ER Marcantonio.

Common Psychosocial Causes   Was a careful case history taken?
Transfer trauma (a recent move that has the individual disoriented)?
Recent death of a spouse or loved one?
Recent stressful event?
Depression and anxiety?
Insomnia?

Common Miscommunication Problems   Did the evaluator assess whether the person could see, hear, and understand questions?
Difficulty understanding English?
Decisions impacted by religious, cultural, or ethnic background?
Low educational or reading level; illiterate?
Difficulty hearing or seeing?

Appendix 6-5
Medications That May Commonly Cause Confusion

Reprinted by permission of the American Bar Association and the American Psychological Association from *Judicial Determination of Capacity of Older Adults in Guardianship Proceedings.*

Class	Uses	Examples of More Problematic Medicines
Anticholinergic	Block the action of the neurotransmitter acetylcholine	Atropine, Scopolamine, and many Antihistamines such as Chlorpheniramin, Cyproheptadine, Dexchlorpheniramine, Diphenhydramine, Hydroxyzine, Promethazine
Antidepressants	Depression	Amitriptyline, Doxepin
AntiParkinson drugs	Parkinson's disease symptoms	Levodopa (L-dopa or Sinemet), Bromocriptine
Antipsychotics	Hallucinations, Delusions	Chlorpromazine, Haloperidol, Thioridazine, Thiothixene
Barbiturates	Sleep and Anxiety	Phenobarbital, Secobarbital

Class	Uses	Examples of More Problematic Medicines
Benzodiazepines	Sleep and Anxiety	Chlordiazepoxide, Diazepam, Flurazepam, Nitrazepam
Histamine-2 (H2) Blockers	Block the action of gastric acid secretion	Cimetidine, Famotidine, Nizatidine, Ranitidine
Nonsteroidal antinflam-matory drugs (NSAIDs)	Pain	Ibuprofen, Indomethacin
Opioids	Pain	Morphine, Propoxyphene, Meperidine
Steroids	Inflammation, Pulmonary disease	Predisone, Dexamethasone, Methylprednisolone

Appendix 6-6
Distinguishing Delirium from Dementia

Reprinted by permission of the American Bar Association and the American Psychological Association from *Judicial Determination of Capacity of Older Adults in Guardianship Proceedings*.

Characteristics	Delirium	Dementia
Onset	Acute	Insidious
Course	Fluctuating	Stable and deteriorating
Duration	Hours to weeks, sometimes longer	Months to years
Attention	Poor	Usually normal
Perception	Hallucinations and misperceptions	Usually normal
Consciousness and orientation	Clouded; disoriented	Clear until late stages
Memory	Poor memory after 1 minute or more	Poor memory after 15 minutes or more, but may be okay in shorter time periods

Note: The most critical factors in distinguishing a temporary cause of impairment from dementia are:

• comes on rather suddenly,

• fluctuates between good and bad,

• problems with attention.

Appendix 6-7
Cognition and Cognitive Testing

Reprinted by permission of the American Bar Association and the American Psychological Association from *Judicial Determination of Capacity of Older Adults in Guardianship Proceedings*.

Cognitive Screening

Cognitive screening tests are useful for giving a general level of overall cognitive impairment. They may be used as an overall screening to determine whether additional testing is needed. They may also be used for individuals with more severe levels of impairment who cannot complete other tests.

Acronym	Screening Test Name	Screening Test Description
BIMC	Blessed Information Memory Concentration Test	33-point scale with subtests of orientation, personal information, current events, recall, and concentration. There is a short version with six items.
Cognistat	The Neurobehavioral Cognitive Status Examination	This screening test examines language, memory, arithmetic, attention, judgment, and reasoning.
MMSE	Mini Mental State Examination	30-point screening instrument that assesses orientation, immediate registration of three words, attention and calculation, short-term recall of three words, language, and visual construction.
MSQ	Mental Status Questionnaire	10-item, 10-point scale assessing orientation to place, time, person, and current events. It has low to modest sensitivity for detecting neurological illness.
7MS	The Seven Minute Screen	This screening instrument combines four tests, each with separate scores of various ranges: recall, verbal fluency, orientation, and clock drawing.
SPMSQ	Short Portable Mental Status Questionnaire	10-point scale scored as a sum of errors on subtests of orientation, location, personal information, current events, and counting backwards. High scores (8–10) equals severe impairment. Race and age corrections to scores are available.

Appendix 6-8
Neuropsychological Assessment and Testing

Reprinted by permission of the American Bar Association and the American Psychological Association from *Judicial Determination of Capacity of Older Adults in Guardianship Proceedings.*

Neuropsychological Testing

A neuropsychological evaluation typically assesses various areas called "domains" with neuroanatomic correlates (see table below). Some of these areas are assessed through observation of the client's presentation and communication during a clinical interview. Most are assessed through tests that have standard instructions, standard scoring, and are referenced to adults of similar age and education to provide performance range that is "norm-referenced."

Domain	Description	Relevance to Capacity	Methods of Assessment
Appearance	√ Grooming, weight, interaction with others	√ Appearance, orientation, and interaction indicate general mental condition and may reveal problems with judgment	√ Observation
Sensory Acuity	√ Ability to hear, see, smell, touch	√ Sensory deficits impact functioning in the environment. √ Sensory deficits may make performance on neuropsychological tests worse and, therefore, should be considered in interpreting scores	√ Observation √ Structured hearing tests √ Structured vision tests
Motor Activity	√ Motor activity (active, agitated, slowed) √ Motor skills (gross and fine) detection of visual, auditory, tactile stimuli	√ Motor deficits impact functioning in the environment. √ Motor deficits may make performance on neuropsychological tests worse and therefore should be considered in interpreting scores	√ Observation √ Finger Tapping √ Grooved Pegboard √ Finger Oscillation Test √ Tactual Performance Test

Domain	Description	Relevance to Capacity	Methods of Assessment
Attention	√ Attend to a stimulus √ Concentrate on a stimulus over brief time periods	√ Basic function necessary for processing information	√ Digit Span Forward and Backward √ Working Memory (from the WMS-III) √ Paced Auditory Serial Attention Test (PASAT) √ Visual Search and Attention Test (VSAT) √ Visual Attention (from the Dementia Rating Scale (DRS)) √ Trails A of the Trail Making Test √ Continuous Performance Test
Memory	√ Working memory: attend to verbal or visual material over short time periods; hold two ideas in mind √ Short-term or recent memory and learning: ability to encode, store, and retrieve information √ Long-term memory: remember information from the past	√ Some memory is important for all decision making. √ Although memory aids can be used, individuals must be able to hold ideas in mind ("working memory") √ Memory is especially important for functioning at home and remembering to perform critical activities (like take medications) and be safe (like turn off stove)	√ Memory Assessment Batteries (from the WMS-III or the Memory Assessment Scales (MAS)) √ Auditory Verbal Learning Test √ Recognition (from the DRS) √ Fuld Object Memory Evaluation √ California Verbal Learning Test (CVLT) √ Hopkins Verbal Learning Test (HVLT) √ Rey Auditory Verbal Learning Test

Domain	Description	Relevance to Capacity	Methods of Assessment
Communication (also called expressive language)	√ Express self in words or writing √ State choices	√ Basic function necessary to convey choices in decision making	√ Communication during testing √ Controlled Oral Word Association Test (commonly called the verbal fluency) √ Boston Diagnostic Aphasia Examination (BDAE) √ Multilingual Aphasia Examination √ Boston Naming Test (BNT)
Understanding (also called receptive language)	√ Understand written, spoken, or visual information	√ Important when making decisions, especially regarding new problems or new treatments √ Critical to understanding the options	√ Understanding during testing √ Boston Diagnostic Aphasia Examination (BDAE) √ Multilingual Aphasia Examination
Arithmetic or Mathematical Skills	√ Understand basic quantities √ Make simple calculations	√ Important for financial decision making √ Important for day to day financial tasks	√ Arithmetic subtest of WAIS-III
Reasoning	√ Compare two choices √ Reason logically about outcomes	√ Critical in almost all decision making	√ Verbal subtests from the WAIS-III, such as Similarities, Comprehension √ Proverbs

Domain	Description	Relevance to Capacity	Methods of Assessment
Visual-Spatial and Visuo-Constructional Reasoning	√ Visual-spatial perception √ Visual problem solving	√ Important for functioning in the home and community √ Essential for driving	√ Performance subtests from WAIS-III, such as Block Design, Object Assembly, Matrix Reasoning √ Hooper Visual Organization Test √ Visual Form Discrimination Test √ Clock Drawing √ Rey-Osterrieth Complex Figure √ Line Bisection √ Bender Visual Motor Gestalt Test √ Tactual Performance Test
Executive Functioning	√ Plan for the future √ Demonstrate judgment √ Inhibit inappropriate responses	√ Essential for most decision making √ Important to avoid undue influence	√ Similarities (from the WAIS-III) √ Trails B of the Trail Making Test (TMT) √ Wisconsin Card Sorting Test √ Stroop Color Word Test √ Delis-Kaplan Executive Function System (DKEFS) √ Mazes √ Tower of London
Insight	√ Acknowledge deficits √ Acknowledge the potential benefit of intervention √ Accept help √ Often considered a part of "executive function"	√ Critical to the use of less restrictive alternatives √ An individual needs to be able to recognize they have a deficit and be willing to accept help in order to use home services	√ Interview √ Comparing observed deficits with the individual's reports of deficits √ Informant reports

Appendix 6-9
Brief Guide to Psychological and Neuropsychological Instruments

Reprinted by permission of the American Bar Association and the American Psychological Association from *Assessment of Older Adults with Diminished Capacity*.

For the purposes of this fact sheet, psychological tests are described in four categories: (1) tests used to evaluate and document symptoms of cognitive impairment; (2) tests used to rate the type and severity of emotional or personality disorder; (3) tests used to detect unusual response styles, or the validity of test taking; and (4) tests used to evaluate specific functional capacities or abilities. A brief guide to cognitive screening instruments is provided at the end of this appendix.

This listing is not meant as an exhaustive or definitive list, but provides an overview of some of the more commonly assessed domains and tests. The number of tests can be somewhat overwhelming; added to this is that evaluators may refer to tests by shortened names or abbreviations. For more information on specific tests, please refer to the reference books noted at the end of this chapter.

A. Tests for Evaluating Cognitive Impairment

A comprehensive psychological or neuropsychological evaluation would typically assess the domains of appearance and motor activity, mood, level of consciousness, attention, memory, language, visual-spatial or constructional ability, reasoning, fund of information, and calculations. Some of these areas are assessed through observation of the client's presentation and communication during a clinical interview. Other areas can be assessed through standardized, norm-referenced tests.

1. Appearance, Orientation, and Motor Activity

Definition: Although typically assessed through observation, not testing, an important part of a comprehensive evaluation is examination of appearance, grooming, weight, motor activity (active, agitated, slowed), and orientation to person, place, time, and current events.

2. Level of consciousness

Definition: Although also typically assessed through observation, not testing, the evaluator will also observe the degree of alertness and general mental confusion, rating as alert, lethargic, or stupor. Additional assessment with basic measure of attention may be necessary.

3. Attention

Definition: Attention concerns the basic ability to attend to a stimulus; also the ability to sustain attention over time, as well as freedom from distractibility.

Tests:

- Digit Span Forward/Digit Span Backward from the Wechsler Adult Intelligence Scale-III (WAIS-III) or the Wechsler Memory Scale-III (WMS-III)

- Working Memory (from the WMS-III)
- Paced Auditory Serial Attention Test (PASAT)
- Visual Search and Attention Test (VSAT)
- Visual Attention (from the Dementia Rating Scale (DRS))
- Trails A of the Trail Making Test

4. Memory and Learning

Definition: Memory assessment involves evaluation of the system by which individuals register, store, retain, and retrieve information in verbal and visual domains.

Tests:

- Memory Assessment Batteries (from the WMS-III or the Memory Assessment Scales (MAS))
- Auditory Verbal Learning Test
- Recall and Recognition (from the DRS)
- Fuld Object Memory Evaluation
- California Verbal Learning Test (CVLT)
- Hopkins Verbal Learning Test (HVLT)

5. Language

Definition: Language includes a number of abilities such as spontaneous speech, the fluency of speech, repetition of speech, naming or word finding, reading, writing, comprehension. The presence of aphasia (difficulty receiving or expressing speech) and thought disordered speech is also noted.

Tests:

- Boston Naming Test (BNT)
- Controlled Oral Word Association Test (commonly called the "FAS")
- Boston Diagnostic Aphasia Examination (BDAE)
- Token Test

6. Executive Function

Definition: The assessment of executive functions concern planning, judgment, purposeful and effective action, concept formation, and volition. This area is often an extremely important aspect of capacity.

Tests:

- Similarities (from the WAIS-III)
- Trails B of the Trail Making Test (TMT)
- Wisconsin Card Sorting Test

- Stroop Color Word Test
- Delis-Kaplan Executive Function System (DKEFS)
- Malloy
- Mazes

7. Visual-Spatial and Visuo-Constructional Reasoning and Abilities

Definition: Visual spatial assessment involves evaluation of visual-spatial perception, problem solving, reasoning, and construction or motor performance involving visual-spatial skills.

Tests:

- Performance subtests from WAIS-III, such as Block Design, Object Assembly, Matrix Reasoning
- Hooper Visual Organization Test
- Visual Form Discrimination Test
- Clock Drawing
- Rey-Osterrieth Complex Figure
- Line Bisection

8. Verbal Reasoning and Abilities

Definition: The assessment of verbal reasoning involves evaluation of logical thinking, practical judgments, and comprehension of relationships. Related abilities are fund of knowledge, which is the extent of information known and retained, and calculation concerning arithmetic skills.

Tests:

- Verbal subtests from the WAIS-III, such as Similarities, Comprehension, Information, Arithmetic
- Proverbs

9. Motor Functions

Definition: Tests of motor function provide basic ability about praxis or motor skills in each hand, which are important for distinguishing observed deficits on tasks involving motor performance from primary (motor) or secondary (central nervous system) deficits.

Tests:

- Finger Tapping
- Grooved Pegboard

B. Tests for Emotional and Personality Functioning

Tests of emotional and personality functioning can provide a more objective means to assess the range and severity of emotional or personal dysfunction.

1. **Mood and Symptoms of Depression, Anxiety, and Psychoses**

   Definition: These scales assess the individual's degree of depressed or anxious mood, and associated symptoms such as insomnia, fatigue, low energy, low appetite, loss of interest or pleasure, irritability, feelings of helplessness, worthlessness, hopelessness, or suicidal ideation. Some scales will also assess the degree of hallucinations, delusions, suspicious or hostile thought processes.

   Tests:

   - Geriatric Depression Scale (GDS)
   - Cornell Scale for Depression in Dementia
   - Dementia Mood Assessment Scale (DMAS)
   - Beck Depression Inventory (BDI)
   - Beck Anxiety Inventory (BAI)
   - Brief Symptom Inventory (BSI)

2. **Personality**

   Definition: Personality inventories are occasionally used in capacity assessment to explore unusual ways of interacting with others and looking at reality that may be impacting sound decision-making. Projective personality tests are relatively less structured and allow the patient open-ended responses. Objective tests in contrast typically provide a question and ask the patient to choose one answer (e.g., "yes" or "no").

   Tests:

   - Rorschach
   - Minnesota Multiphasic Personality Inventory-2 (MMPI)
   - Profile of Mood States (POMS)

C. **Tests of Effort, Motivation, or Response Style**

These measures, also referred to as validity tests, are structured in such a way to detect inconsistent or unlikely response patterns indicative of attempts to exaggerate cognitive problems. They serve as one type of evidence permitting the clinician to judge the validity of the overall cognitive testing. Generally they detect test-taking response patterns that deviate from chance responding or from norms for established cognitively impaired clinical populations like AD. If the tests are positive, they suggest an intentional (or in some cases subconscious) test-taking approach to exaggerate deficits. It remains a clinical judgment as to how to interpret the clinical meaning of the test-taking bias/exaggeration. In some cases, they may reflect malingering for monetary secondary gain, whereas in others they may indicate a factitious disorder or sometimes a somatoform disorder.

Tests of validity may be used when the examiner is concerned that the individual has a reason to gain from "faking bad" on the test, such as in disability claims. Older adults who are receiving capacity evaluation are most likely to be giving maximal effort to perform at their highest level, in which case formal tests of validity are probably not indicated.

1. **Validity**

    Definition: Validity tests are structured in such a way to detect inconsistent or unlikely response patterns indicative of attempts to exaggerate cognitive dysfunction.

    Tests:

    - Test of Memory Malingering (TOMM)
    - 21 Item Test
    - 15 Item Test
    - CVLT-II Forced Choice

D. Tests for Evaluating Specific Capacities or Abilities

When capacity or competency is specifically in question, a comprehensive evaluation would include direct assessment of the area in question. We include here instruments designed for clinical (not research) use. As these tests are more recently developed, we include a more detailed description of the instruments. Specific information on reliability and validity relevant to the Daubert standard of scientific admissibility can be found in the test manuals.

1. Adult Functional Adaptive Behavior Scale (AFABS)

Primary Reference: P.S. Pierce, Adult Functional Adaptive Behavior Scale: Manual of Directions (1989).

Area Assessed: Functional Abilities for Independent Living

Description: The Adult Functional Adaptive Behavior Scale (AFABS) was developed to assist in the assessment of ADL and IADL functions in the elderly to evaluate their capacity for personal responsibility and the matching of a client to a placement setting. The AFABS consists of 14 items. Six items rate ADLs: eating, ambulation, toileting, dressing, grooming, and managing (keeping clean) personal area. Two items tap IADLs: managing money and managing health needs. Six items tap cognitive and social functioning: socialization, environmental orientation (ranging from able to locate room up through able to travel independently in the community), reality orientation (aware of person, place, time, and current events), receptive speech communication, expressive communication, and memory. Items are rated on four levels: 0.0 representing a lack of the capacity, 0.5 representing some capacity with assistance, 1.0 representing some capacity without assistance, and 1.5 representing independent functioning in that area. Individual scores are summed to receive a total score in adaptive functioning.

The AFABS assesses adaptive functioning through interviewing an informant well-acquainted with the functioning of the individual in question. The informant data is combined with the examiner's observation of and interaction with the client to arrive at final ratings. The AFABS is designed for relatively easy and brief administration (approximately 15 minutes). The author recommends it be administered only by professionals experienced in psychological and functional assessment, specifically a psychologist, occupational therapist, or psychometrician, although research with the AFABS has also utilized psychiatric nurses and social workers trained in its administration.

2. **Aid to Capacity Evaluation (ACE)**

Primary Reference: Edward Etchells et al., Assessment of Patients Capacity to Consent to Treatment, 14 J. Gen. Internal Med. 27–34 (1990).

Area Assessed: Medical Decision-Making

Description: The ACE is a semi-structured assessment interview that addresses seven facets of capacity for an actual medical decision (not a standardized vignette): the ability to understand (1) the medical problem, (2) the treatment, (3) the alternatives to treatment, and (4) the option of refusing treatment; (5) the ability to perceive consequences of (6a) accepting treatment and (6b) refusing treatment; and (7) the ability to make a decision not substantially based on hallucinations, delusions, or depression. These reflect legal standards in Ontario, Canada but also correspond to U.S. legal standards.

3. **Capacity Assessment Tool (CAT)**

Primary Reference: M.T. Carney et al., The Development and Piloting of a Capacity Assessment Tool, 12 J. Clinical Ethics 17–23 (2001).

Area Assessed: Medical Decision-Making

Description: The CAT proposes to evaluate capacity based on six abilities: communication, understanding choices, comprehension of risks and benefits, insight, decision/choice process, and judgment. It uses a structured interview format to assess capacity to choose between two options in an actual treatment situation; as such, it does not use a hypothetical vignette.

4. **Capacity to Consent to Treatment Interview (CCTI)**

Primary Reference: Daniel C. Marson et al., Assessing the Competency of Patients with Alzheimer's Disease Under Different Legal Standards, 52 Arch. Neurol. 949–954 (1995).

Area Assessed: Medical Decision-Making

Description: The CCTI is based on two clinical vignettes; a neoplasm condition and a cardiac condition. Information about each condition and related treatment alternatives is presented at a fifth to sixth grade reading level with low syntactic complexity. Vignettes are presented orally and in writing; participants are then presented questions to assess their decisional abilities in terms of understanding, appreciation, reasoning, and expression of choice.

5. **Competency Interview Schedule (CIS)**

Primary Reference: G. Bean et al., The Assessment of Competence to Make a Treatment Decision: An Empirical Approach, 41 Can. J. Psych. 85–92 (1996).

Area Assessed: Medical Decision-Making

Description: The CIS is a 15-item interview designed to assess consent capacity for electro-convulsive therapy (ECT). Patients referred for ECT receive information about their diagnosis and treatment alternatives by the treating clinician, and the CIS then assesses decisional abilities based on responses to the 15 items.

6. Decision Assessment Measure

Primary Reference: J.G. Wong et al., The Capacity of People with a "Mental Disability" to Make a Health Care Decision, 30 Psych. Med. 295–306 (2000).

Area Assessed: Medical Decision-Making

Description: Wong et al., working in England, developed a measure that references incapacity criteria in England and Wales (understanding, reasoning, and communicating a choice), based on methodology by Thomas Grisso et al. (*The MacArthur Treatment Competence Study: II. Measures of Abilities Related to Competence to Consent to Treatment*, 19(2) L. & Human Behavior 127–148 (1995)). Their instrument also assesses the ability to retain material because it is one of the legal standards for capacity in England and Wales (though not in the United States).

A standardized vignette regarding blood drawing is used to assess paraphrased recall, recognition, and non-verbal demonstration of understanding (pointing to the correct information on a sheet with both correct information and distracter/incorrect information).

7. Decision-Making Instrument for Guardianship (DIG)

Primary Reference: S.J. Anderer, Developing An Instrument to Evaluate the Capacity of Elderly Persons to Make Personal Care and Financial Decisions (1997) (Unpubl. doctoral dissertation, Allegheny Univ. of Health Sciences).

Area Assessed: Self Care, Home Care, Financial, (Guardianship)

Description: The Decision-Making Instrument for Guardianship (DIG) was developed to evaluate the abilities of individuals to make decisions in everyday situations often the subject of guardianship proceedings. The instrument consists of eight vignettes describing situations involving problems in eight areas: hygiene, nutrition, health care, residence, property acquisition, routine money management in property acquisition, major expenses in property acquisition, and property disposition. Examinees are read a brief vignette describing these situations in the second person. Detailed scoring criteria are used to assign points for aspects of problem solving including defining the problem, generating alternatives, consequential thinking, and complex/comparative thinking. The DIG is carefully standardized. Standard instructions, vignettes, questions, and prompts are provided in the manual. In addition, detailed scoring criteria are provided. Sheets with simplified lists of salient points of each vignette, provided in large type, help to standardize vignette administration and emphasize the assessment of problem solving and not reading comprehension or memory. Vignettes are kept simple, easy to understand, and are brief.

8. Direct Assessment of Functional Status (DAFS)

Primary Reference: David A. Loewenstein et al., A New Scale for the Assessment of Functional Status in Alzheimer's Disease and Related Disorders, 44 J. Gerontology: Psych. Sci. 114–121 (1989).

Area Assessed: Functional Abilities for Independent Living

Description: The Direct Assessment of Functional Status (DAFS) was designed to assess functional abilities in individuals with dementing illnesses. The scale assesses seven areas: time orientation (16 points), communication abilities (including telephone and mail; 17 points), transportation (requiring reading of road signs; 13 points), financial skills (including identifying and counting currency, writing a check and balancing a checkbook; 21 points), shopping skills (involving grocery shopping; 16 points), eating skills (10 points), dressing and grooming skills (13 points). The composite functional score has a maximum of 93 points, exclusive of the driving subscale, which is considered optional. The DAFS requires that the patient attempt to actually perform each item (e.g., is given a telephone and asked to dial the operator). The entire assessment is estimated to require 30–35 minutes to complete. Any psychometrically trained administrator can administer the scale. The DAFS has been used for staging functional impairment in dementia, from one to three, in a group of 205 individuals with probable Alzheimer's disease.

9. Financial Capacity Instrument (FCI)

Primary Reference: Daniel C. Marson et al., Assessment of Financial Capacity in Patients with Alzheimer's Disease: A Prototype Instrument, 57 Arch. Neurol. 877–884 (2000).

Area Assessed: Financial

Description: The Financial Capacity Instrument (FCI) was designed to assess everyday financial activities and abilities. The instrument assesses six domains of financial activity: basic monetary skills, financial conceptual knowledge, cash transactions, checkbook management, bank statement management, and financial judgment. The FCI is reported to require between 30–50 minutes to administer, depending on the cognitive level of the examinee. The FCI uses an explicit protocol for administration and scoring.

10. Hopemont Capacity Assessment Interview (HCAI)

Primary Reference: Barry Edelstein et al., *Assessment of Capacity to Make Financial and Medical Decisions* (1993) (paper presented at Toronto meeting of the American Psychological Association, August 1993).

Area Assessed: Financial, Medical Decision-Making

Description: The Hopemont Capacity Assessment Interview (HCAI) is a semi-structured interview in two sections. The first section is for assessing capacity to make medical decisions. The second section is for assessing capacity to make financial decisions and will be discussed here. In the interview the examinee is first presented with concepts of choice, cost, and benefits and these concepts are reviewed with the examinee through questions and answers. The examinee is then presented medical or financial scenarios. For each scenario the individual is asked basic questions about what he or she has heard, and then asked to explain costs and benefits, to make a choice, and to explain the reasoning behind that choice. The HCAI uses a semi-structured format. General instructions are provided. Specific standardized introductions, scenarios, and follow-up questions are on the rating form.

11. Independent Living Scales (ILS)

Primary Reference: Patricia A. Loeb, Independent Living Scales (1996).

Areas Assessed: Care of Home, Health Care, Financial (Guardianship)

Description: The Independent Living Scales (ILS) is an individually administered instrument developed to assess abilities of the elderly associated with caring for oneself and/or for one's property. The early version of the ILS was called the Community Competence Scale (CCS). The CCS was constructed specifically to be consistent with legal definitions, objectives, and uses, in order to enhance its value for expert testimony about capacities of the elderly in legal guardianship cases. The ILS consists of 70 items in five subscales: Memory/Orientation, Managing Money, Managing Home and Transportation, Health and Safety, and Social Adjustment. The five subscales may be summed to obtain an overall score, which is meant to reflect the individual's capacity to function independently overall. Two factors may be derived from items across the five subscales: Problem Solving and Performance/Information. The ILS has extensive information on norms, reliability, and validity.

12. MacArthur Competence Assessment Tool - Treatment (MACCAT-T)

Primary Reference: Thomas Grisso & Paul S. Applebaum, Assessing Competence to Consent to Treatment (1998).

Area Assessed: Medical Decision-Making

Description: The MacCAT-T utilizes a semi-structured interview to guide the clinician through an assessment of the capacity to make an actual treatment decision. It does not use a standardized vignette. Patients receive information about their condition, including the name of the disorder, its features and course, then are asked to "Please describe to me your understanding of what I just said." Incorrect or omitted information is cued with a prompt (e.g., "What is the condition called?"), and if still incorrect or omitted, presented again. A similar disclosure occurs for the treatments, including the risks and benefits of each treatment alternative. Next, patients are asked if they have any reason to doubt the information and to describe that. They are then asked to express a choice and to answer several questions that explicate their reasoning process, including comparative and consequential reasoning and logical consistency.

13. Multidimensional Functional Assessment Questionnaire (MFAQ)

Primary Reference: Center for the Study of Aging and Human Development, Multidimensional Functional Assessment: The OARS Methodology (1978).

Area Assessed: Functional Abilities for Independent Living

Description: The Multidimensional Functional Assessment Questionnaire (MFAQ) was developed to provide a reliable and valid method for characterizing elderly individuals and for describing elderly populations. The MFAQ supersedes the nearly identical Community Survey Questionnaire (CSQ, a predecessor which also was developed by the Duke Center). Both instruments frequently have been called the "OARS," in reference to the program that developed the instrument throughout the 1970s. The MFAQ or the CSQ was already in use by well over 50 service centers, researchers, or practitioners nationally when the MFAQ was published (1978). Part A provides information in five areas of functioning, including activities of daily living. The Activities of Daily Living (ADL) dimension assesses 14 functions including both instrumental and physical ADLs. *Instrumental ADLs are*: use telephone, use transportation, shopping, prepare meals, do housework, take medicine, handle money. *Physical ADLs are*: eat, dress oneself, care for own appearance, walk, get in/out of bed, bath, getting to bathroom, continence. Part B of the MFAQ assesses the individual's utilization of services, that is, whether and to what extent the examinee has received assistance from various community programs, agencies, relatives, or friends, especially within the latest six months. Questioning also includes the examinee's perceived need for the various services.

14. Philadelphia Geriatric Center Multilevel Assessment Inventory (MAI)

Primary Reference: M. Powell Lawton & Miriam Moss, Philadelphia Geriatric Center Multilevel Assessment.

Instrument: Manual for Full-length MAI (undated).

Area Assessed: Functional Abilities for Independent Living

Description: The Philadelphia Geriatric Center Multilevel Assessment Inventory (MAI) was designed to assess characteristics of the elderly relevant for determining their needs for services and placement in residential settings. The MAI is a structured interview procedure that obtains descriptive information about an elderly respondent related to seven domains. Each of the domains (except one) is sampled by interview questions in two or more subclasses, which the authors call sub-indexes. The full-length MAI consists of 165 items; the middle length MAI has 38 items, and the short-form has 24 items. The domains assessed are physical health, cognitive, activities of daily living, time use, personal adjustment, social interaction, and perceived environment. The MAI manual provides considerable structure for the process of the interview, sequence and content of questions, and scoring. It describes criteria for 1 to 5 rating of each of the domains, but these criteria are not tied specifically to item scores. The manual discusses general considerations for interviewing elderly individuals and dealing with special problems of test administration with this population (e.g., dealing with limited hearing or vision).

E. Cognitive Screening Tests

Cognitive screening tests are useful for giving a general level of overall cognitive impairment, but they are notoriously insensitive to deficits in single domains. They may be used as an overall screening to determine whether additional testing is needed. They may also be used for individuals with more severe levels of impairment who cannot complete other tests.

1. Blessed Information-Memory-Concentration Test (BIMC): The BIMC is a 33-point scale with subtests of orientation, personal information, current events, recall, and concentration. There is a short version with six items. It has adequate test-retest reliability and correlation with other measures of cognitive impairment.

2. Mental Status Questionnaire (MSQ): The MSQ is a 10-item, 10-point scale assessing orientation to place, time, person, and current events. It has low to modest sensitivity for detecting neurological illness.

3. Mini Mental State Examination (MMSE): The MMSE is a 30-point screening instrument that assesses orientation, immediate registration of three words, attention and calculation, short-term recall of three words, language, and visual construction. The MMSE is widely used and has adequate reliability and validity. Positive findings require more in-depth evaluation. Limitations of the MMSE, discussed in Chapter IV, include the potential for false positives or false negatives, and the association of MMSE scores with age, education, and ethnicity. Longer versions and telephone versions of the MMSE are available.

4. The Seven Minute Screen (7MS): This screening instrument consists of four subtests: recall, verbal fluency, orientation, and clock drawing. It has adequate test-retest reliability and inter-rater reliability.

5. Short Portable Mental Status Questionnaire (SPMSQ): The SPMSQ is scored as a sum of errors on subtests of orientation, location, personal information, current events, and counting backwards. Race and age corrections to scores are available.

F.   Key Test Reference Books

Thomas Grisso et al., Evaluating Competencies: Forensic Assessments and Instruments (2d ed. 2002).

Asenath LaRue, Aging and Neuropsychological Assessment (1992).

Muriel D. Lezak, Neuropsychological Assessment (3d ed. 1995).

Peter A. Lichetenberg ed., Handbook of Assessment in Clinical Gerontology (1999).

Otfried Spreen & Esther Strauss, A Compendium of Neuropsychological Tests: Administration, Norms, and Commentary (2d ed. 1998).

Appendix 6-10
Everyday Functioning and Functional Assessment

Reprinted by permission of the American Bar Association and the American Psychological Association from *Judicial Determination of Capacity of Older Adults in Guardianship Proceedings*.

What Is "Function?" How do Judges and Clinicians Think Differently?

A comprehensive assessment of capacity should include a "functional assessment." When the law refers to "function" it often means someone's thinking and decision-making, as well as everyday behavior where the person lives. When clinicians refer to "function" they usually mean only the everyday behavior, whereas thinking and decision making is assessed separately as "cognition."

How Do Clinicians Divide Everyday Functioning? What Are ADLs and IADLs?

Clinicians often divide everyday function into the "Activities of Daily Living" (ADL) and the "Instrumental Activities of Daily Living" (IADL). There is fairly good agreement on the ADLs as comprising dressing, eating, toileting, transferring or moving from one sitting position to another, walking or mobility, and bathing. There is less agreement on what are the main categories of IADLs and how to divide them.

How Is Functioning Assessed by Clinicians? Informal and Formal Assessments of Capacity

Functioning can be assessed through informal means, such as observing the individual, and asking the individual, family, and staff questions, or through formal testing, such as that performed by an occupational therapist. Nurses, social workers, and psychologists are often prepared to assess everyday functioning.

What Tests Are Used to Assess Everyday Functioning? ADL Rating Scales and Capacity Tools

There are two main ways that functioning is formally assessed. One way is through ADL and IADL rating scales. These are often used by nurses and social workers and are usually brief check lists for categorizing everyday functioning. Similar and more sophisticated tools are used by occupational therapists who tend to directly assess and observe ADL/IADL performance in their evaluations. ADL and IADL rating scales have been available for more than 30 years.

ADL/IADL Rating Scales include:

- Adult Functional Adaptive Behavior Scale (AFABS)
- Barthel Index
- Direct Assessment of Functional Status (DAFS)
- Functional Independence Measure (FIM)
- Index of ADL ("Katz")
- Kenny Self Care Evaluation
- Multidimensional Functional Assessment Questionnaire (MFAQ)
- Philadelphia Geriatric Center Multilevel Assessment Inventory (MAI)
- Physical Self-Maintenance Scale

Another approach to functional assessment is instruments designed specifically to assess legal capacities. These are formal testing instruments designed specifically to assess capacity in terms of legal definitions. Such tools have only recently been developed, since the 1990s, and are summarized in the following table. They are called "tools" because it is not possible to have an exact "test" of capacity. Capacity is a professional, clinical, and, ultimately, legal judgment. Since some of these tests are newly developed, not all meet the "Daubert standard" of scientific admissibility.

Acronym	Capacity Tool Name	Description
ACE	Aid to Capacity Evaluation	Semi-structured interview for capacity to consent to treatment; Developed in Canada.
CAT	Capacity Assessment Tool	Structured interview to assess capacity to choose between two treatment options.
CCTI	Capacity to Consent to Treatment Interview	Two clinical vignettes are used to assess capacity to consent to medical treatment in terms of legal standards of understanding, appreciation, reasoning, and expression of choice.
CIS	Competency Interview Schedule	A 15-item interview for capacity to consent to electro-convulsive-therapy (ECT).
DAM	Decision Assessment Measure	Assesses capacity to consent to medical treatment through a vignette regarding blood draw. Developed in England.
DIG	Decision-Making Instrument for Guardianship	Eight vignettes evaluate capacity to make decisions about hygiene, nutrition, health care, residence, property acquisition, routine money management in property acquisition, major expenses in property acquisition, and property disposition.
FCI	Financial Capacity Instrument	Structured instrument assesses six domains of financial activity: basic monetary skills, financial conceptual knowledge, cash transactions, checkbook management, bank statement management, and financial judgment.
HCAI	Hopemont Capacity Assessment Interview	Semi structured interview for medical and financial decisions. Uses two vignettes for each.
ILS	Independent Living Scales	Structured instrument with 70 items in five subscales: memory/orientation, managing money, managing home and transportation, health and safety, and social adjustment. Can be summed to reflect the capacity to function independently.
MacCAT-T	MacArthur Competence Assessment Tool - Treatment	Semi-structured interview to assess medical decision making in terms of four legal standards.

Appendix 6-11
Means to Enhance Capacity

Reprinted by permission of the American Bar Association and the American Psychological Association from *Judicial Determination of Capacity of Older Adults in Guardianship Proceedings*.

Cause of Confusion	Possible Intervention
Alcohol or other substances intoxification	Detoxification; supplement diet or other intake needs
Altered blood pressure	Treat underlying cause of blood pressure anomaly with medication or other treatment
Altered low blood sugar	Management of blood sugar through diet or medication
Anxiety	Treatment with medications and/or psychotherapy; support groups
Bereavement; Recent death of a spouse or loved one	Support; counseling by therapist or clergy; support group; medications to assist in short term problems (e.g., sleep, depression)
Bipolar disorder	Treatment with medications and/or psychotherapy; support groups
Brain tumor	Surgery and medication
Delirium	Obtain standard labs; obtain brain scan if indicated; assess vitals; treat underlying cause; monitor and reassess over time
Dementia	Treatment with medications for dementia; simplify environment; provide multiple clues within environment; use step-by-step communication
Depression	Treatment with medications and/or psychotherapy; add pleasurable activities to day; ECT if indicated; support groups
Developmental disability	Education and training
Difficulty hearing	Use hearing amplifiers; have hearing evaluated; provide hearing aids; write information down; repeat information; slow down speech; speak clearly and distinctly
Difficulty seeing	Use magnifying glass; have sight evaluated; provide glasses; provide spoken information; repeat information; ensure sufficient lighting; use large print; have access to Braille materials
Difficulty understanding English	Use translator

Cause of Confusion	Possible Intervention
Head injury	Treatments for acute effects (e.g., bleed, pressure, swelling) as necessary; monitoring over time; rehabilitative speech, physical, occupational therapies
Infection (e.g., urinary, influenza, pneumonia, meningitis)	Treat underlying infection with antibiotic or other treatment
Insomnia	Sleep hygiene practices (e.g., limit caffeine, light exercise, limit naps); medications
Liver or kidney disease	Treatment of underlying illness with medication, dialysis, surgery
Loneliness	Social and recreational activities; support groups
Low educational or reading level; illiterate	Provide information in simple language without "talking down"; provide information in multiple formats
Malnutrition or dehydration	IV fluids; fluid/food by mouth; food supplements; food by feeding tube
Mania	Treatment with medications and/or psychotherapy; support groups
Medications and sudden medication withdrawal	Review of medications by clinical pharmacist or specialist; slow one-by-one tapers or changes of medications
Poor heart or lung function (e.g., hypoxia)	Treatment of underlying condition with medication, surgery, supplemental oxygen
Post surgical confusion (usually related to anesthesia or pain medicines)	Monitoring and reassessment over time; try alternative medications and treatments for pain management
Recent stressful event; depression and anxiety	Support, counseling by therapist or clergy; support group; medications to treat symptoms
Religious, cultural, or ethnic background	Sensitivity to religious, cultural, and ethnic traditions; inquire about views and needs; involve professional from similar background
Schizophrenia; hallucinations or delusions	Treatment with medications for schizophrenia; simplify environment; provide support
Transfer trauma (a recent move that has the individual disoriented)	Monitoring over time; re-orientation to environment
Transient ischemic attacks (TIA)	Treatment of risk factors to prevent future recurrence
Urinary or fecal retention	Treat underlying cause of retention through medication or surgery
Vitamin deficiency; imbalances in electrolytes and blood levels	Vitamin or electrolyte supplement; balanced diet; diet supplements

Appendix 6-12
Additional Resources

Assessment of Older Adults with Diminished Capacity: A Handbook for Lawyers (Washington, DC: American Bar Association, 2005).

Judicial Determination of Capacity of Older Adults in Guardianship Proceedings (Washington, DC: American Bar Association, 2006).

Stephen J. Anderer, *Determining Competency in Guardianship Proceedings* (Washington, DC: American Bar Association, 1990).

Charles P. Sabatino and Suzanna L. Basinger, *Competency: Reforming Our Legal Fictions*, 6 J. MENTAL HEALTH & AGING 119 (2000).

George H. Zimny, *Guardianship of the Elderly* (New York: Springer Publishing Co., 1998).

Michael Smyer, et. al. (eds.), *Older Adults' Decision-Making and the Law* (New York: Springer Publishing Co., 1996).

Jennifer Moye, *Evaluating the Capacity of Older Adults: Psychological Models and Tools*, NAELA QUARTERLY (Summer 2004).

Jeffrey S. Janofsky, *Assessing Competency in the Elderly*, 45:10 GERIATRICS 45 (October 1990).

Thomas Grisso, et al. *Evaluating Competencies: Forensic Assessments and Instruments* (New York: Plenum Press, 2002).

Marshall B. Kapp, *Evaluating Decision Making Capacity in the Elderly: A Review of Recent Literature*, 2 J. ELDER ABUSE AND NEGLECT 15 (1990).

Marshall B. Kapp and D. Mossman, *Measuring Decisional Capacity: Cautions on the Construction of a Capacimeter*, 2:1 PSYCH., PUB. POL. & LAW 73 (1996).

Lawrence A. Frolik, *Promoting Judicial Acceptance and Use of Limited Guardianship*, 31 STETSON L. REV. 735 (2001).

CHAPTER 7:
Appointment of Guardians

7.1
Scope of this Chapter

This chapter summarizes the substantive law governing the appointment of an individual, corporation, agency, or official as the general guardian, guardian of the person, or guardian of the estate of an incapacitated respondent who is being represented by an attorney who has been appointed as the respondent's *guardian ad litem* pursuant to G.S. 35A-1107.

The powers and duties of general guardians, guardians of the person, and guardians of the estate are briefly summarized in Chapter 1.

The procedural law governing hearings to appoint a guardian for an incapacitated respondent is discussed in Chapters 3 through 5. Chapter 5 also discusses the appointment of interim guardians for allegedly incapacitated respondents in adult guardianship proceedings.

Procedures governing the removal of a guardian, the appointment of successor guardians, and the modification or termination of guardianship orders are discussed in Chapter 10.

This manual does not discuss the appointment of ancillary guardians pursuant to G.S. 35A-1280.

7.2
Types of Guardians That May Be Appointed

Article 5 of G.S. Chapter 35A authorizes the Clerk of Superior Court to appoint

- a general guardian of an incapacitated adult,
- a guardian of the person of an incapacitated adult,
- a guardian of the estate of an incapacitated adult.

Depending on the nature and extent of a respondent's incapacity, needs, assets, income, and liabilities, the Clerk may determine that it is appropriate to appoint a general guardian for the respondent; to appoint separate persons or entities as the guardian of the ward's person and guardian of the ward's estate; to appoint only a guardian of the person for the respondent; to appoint only a guardian of the estate for the respondent; or to create a limited guardianship that allows the respondent to retain certain legal rights and limits the guardian's statutory powers.

General guardian. A general guardian is a guardian who has the authority of a guardian of the person and a guardian of the estate of an incapacitated ward. G.S. 35A-1202(7).

Practice Note: The Clerk should not appoint a general guardian for a ward unless the ward has or will have an estate that should be managed by a guardian, the ward needs a guardian of his or her person, and the Clerk determines that the same person or persons should exercise authority as guardian of the ward's person and estate.

Guardian of the person. A guardian of the person is a guardian who is appointed solely for the purpose of performing duties relating to the care, custody, and control of an incapacitated ward. G.S. 35A-1202(10).

Practice Note: Appointment of a guardian of the ward's person rather than appointment of a general guardian or without appointment of a guardian of the ward's estate is appropriate if the ward does not have an estate that needs to be managed by a guardian but needs a guardian to make decisions regarding his or her care.

Guardian of the estate. A guardian of the estate is a guardian who is appointed solely for the purpose of managing the property, estate, and business affairs of an incapacitated ward. G.S. 35A-1202(9).

Practice Note: The Clerk should not appoint a general guardian or guardian of the estate for a ward unless the ward has or will have an estate that should be managed by a guardian. If the only income and assets of a ward consist of Social Security or SSI benefits or other public assistance payments, management of the ward's income and assets through a representative payee generally is more appropriate than appointment of a guardian of the ward's estate under G.S. Chapter 35A.

Ancillary guardian. An ancillary guardian is a guardian of the estate who is appointed pursuant to Article 12 of G.S. Chapter 35A on behalf of a nonresident ward when a general guardian, guardian of the estate, or similar fiduciary has been appointed for the ward under the laws of another state and the ward has an ownership or other interest in real or personal property in North Carolina. This manual does not discuss the appointment of ancillary guardians under G.S. 35A-1280 because the respondent in a proceeding to appoint an ancillary guardian is not represented by an attorney who is appointed as a *guardian ad litem* under G.S. 35A-1107.

Interim guardian. An interim guardian is a temporary guardian who is appointed pursuant to Article 1 of G.S. Chapter 35A to protect an allegedly incapacitated respondent's well-being or estate from imminent harm. G.S. 35A-1114. The appointment of interim guardians is discussed in Chapter 5.

Practice Note: G.S. 35A-1114 does not authorize the appointment of an "interim" or "emergency" guardian after the Clerk has determined that a respondent is incapacitated and has appointed a guardian for the respondent—even in cases in which there is an emergency due to the guardian's death, resignation, removal, or failure or refusal to protect the ward. The Clerk, however, may enter an emergency order under G.S. 35A-1291 to protect the ward or the ward's property in these situations.

7.3
Legal Standards for Appointment of a Guardian

A. Incapacity

The Clerk may not appoint a guardian for a respondent in an adult guardianship proceeding unless the respondent has been adjudicated incapacitated. *In re Efird*, 114 N.C. App. 638 (1994).

B. Best Interest of the Ward

The Clerk's decisions regarding the appointment of a guardian for an incapacitated respondent should be based on the respondent's "best interests" as determined by the Clerk. *See* G.S. 35A-1212(a)(3); G.S. 35A-1212.1.

When appointing a guardian for an incapacitated respondent, the Clerk should appoint the person, corporation, agency, or official who will be the most suitable, qualified, and responsible guardian for the respondent. *See* G.S. 35A-1212(a)(3); G.S. 35A-1212.1.

C. Other Statutory Considerations and Requirements

The Clerk should not appoint a guardian for an incapacitated respondent unless it is clear that doing so will give the respondent a fuller capacity for exercising his or her rights. G.S. 35A-1201(a)(4).

In appointing a guardian for an incapacitated respondent, the Clerk should create a "limited guardianship" whenever the nature and extent of the respondent's incapacity makes creation of a limited guardianship appropriate. *See* G.S. 35A-1212(a).

The Clerk may not appoint a person, corporation, agency, or official as the guardian for an incapacitated respondent unless the prospective guardian is legally qualified to serve as the respondent's guardian and meets all of the applicable requirements set forth in G.S. Chapter 35A.

7.4
Procedure for Appointing a Guardian

A. Nature of Proceeding

The aspect of a guardianship proceeding involving the appointment of a guardian for an incapacitated respondent generally is treated as an "estate" matter, rather than a special proceeding. *See In re Simmons*, 266 N.C. 702 (1966); *In re Bidstrup*, 55 N.C. App. 394 (1982).

Practice Note: Because the appointment of a guardian is treated as an "estate" matter, the appeal of an order appointing a guardian for an incapacitated adult is governed by G.S. 1-301.3 except with respect to appeals involving the issue of the respondent's incapacity. Appeals in adult guardianship proceedings are discussed in Chapter 9 of this manual.

B. Authority of the Clerk, Jury, and Judge to Appoint Guardians

The Clerk of Superior Court has exclusive jurisdiction with respect to the appointment of guardians for incapacitated adults.

Issues regarding who should be appointed as the guardian of an incapacitated adult may not be determined by a jury in an adult guardianship proceeding.

If the Clerk's order appointing a guardian is appealed to the Superior Court, the Superior Court Judge may reverse the Clerk's order appointing a guardian in cases involving legal error or abuse of judicial discretion and remand the case to the Clerk for further proceedings, but may not appoint a person, corporation, disinterested public agent, or public guardian as the respondent's guardian. *See In re Simmons*, 266 N.C. 702 (1966).

C. Role of the Respondent's Attorney or *Guardian ad Litem*

If an attorney has been appointed as a respondent's *guardian ad litem* pursuant to G.S. 35A-1107, the attorney has not been discharged, and the respondent is adjudicated incapacitated, the attorney continues to represent the incapacitated respondent until a guardian is appointed for the respondent. G.S. 35A-1107(b).

The respondent's attorney or *guardian ad litem* may recommend, on behalf of the respondent, that a particular person be appointed or not be appointed as the respondent's guardian, may present evidence, on behalf of the respondent, to the Clerk regarding the appointment of a guardian for the respondent, and may examine and cross-examine witnesses who testify with respect to the appointment of a guardian for the respondent.

The respondent's *guardian ad litem* must make the respondent's express wishes with respect to appointment of a guardian known to the Clerk and *may* make recommendations to the Clerk regarding the appointment of a guardian for the respondent if the attorney determines that those recommendations are in the respondent's best interest and are consistent with the attorney's statutory and professional obligations. See G.S. 35A-1107(b).

If the respondent's attorney or *guardian ad litem* determines that creation of a limited guardianship is in the respondent's best interest, he or she may make recommendations to the Clerk regarding the rights, powers, and privileges that should be retained by the respondent and the extent to which the guardian's statutory powers should be limited if the attorney determines that those recommendations are in the respondent's best interest and are consistent with the attorney's statutory and professional obligations. See G.S. 35A-1107(b).

The role and responsibilities of the respondent's attorney or *guardian ad litem* are discussed in more detail in Chapter 2.

D. Hearing

Before appointing a guardian for an incapacitated adult, the Clerk must hold a hearing to determine

- the respondent's assets, liabilities, and needs;
- the nature and extent of the needed guardianship;

- whether a "limited guardianship" is appropriate and feasible; and
- who, in the Clerk's discretion, can most suitably serve as the respondent's guardian. G.S. 35A-1212(a).

The hearing regarding the appointment of a guardian for an incapacitated respondent may be combined with the hearing regarding the respondent's incapacity or may be held following the adjudication of the respondent's incapacity.

Unless a guardianship proceeding has been transferred to another county pursuant to G.S. 35A-1205 following the adjudication of a respondent's incapacity, a hearing to appoint a guardian for an incapacitated respondent is held in the same county in which the order adjudicating the respondent's incapacity was entered.

Practice Note: The transfer of an adult guardianship proceeding to another county under G.S. 35A-1205 is discussed in Chapter 3 of this manual.

E. Evidence, Evaluations, and Reports

Scope of hearing. The Clerk must "make such inquiry and receive such evidence as the Clerk deems necessary to determine . . . the nature and extent of the needed guardianship . . . and who, in the Clerk's discretion, can most suitably serve as the [respondent's] guardian. . . ." G.S. 35A-1212.

Rules of evidence. Although hearings regarding the appointment of a guardian for an incapacitated respondent often are uncontested or informal, the North Carolina Rules of Evidence are applicable.

Recording the hearing. Because an appeal from a Clerk's order appointing a guardian for an incapacitated adult is reviewed by the Superior Court "on the record," the Clerk is required, upon request of a party, to make an electronic recording of the portion of a guardianship proceeding involving the appointment of a guardian for an incapacitated adult. *See* G.S. 1-301.3(f).

Practice Note: The attorney who has been appointed as the respondent's *guardian ad litem* should request the Clerk to record the entire hearing in an adult guardianship proceeding.

Multidisciplinary evaluation. If a current multidisciplinary evaluation (MDE) is not available, the Clerk may, on the Clerk's own motion or on the request of any party, order that an MDE be performed to assist the Clerk in determining the nature and extent of the respondent's incapacity, the nature and extent of the needed guardianship, whether a "limited guardianship" is appropriate and feasible, and the guardianship program or plan that should be implemented for the respondent. G.S. 35A-1212(b); G.S. 35A-1111(a).

Practice Note: The procedure for requesting a multidisciplinary evaluation is discussed in Chapter 5 of this manual. The requirements for preparing a multidisciplinary evaluation are discussed in Chapter 6 of this manual.

Reports and recommendations by designated human services agencies. The Clerk may order a designated state or local human services agency to prepare a report evaluating the suitability of a prospective guardian and recommending the most suitable and appropriate party or person to serve as an incapacitated adult's guardian. G.S. 35A-1212(c).

Practice Note: G.S. Chapter 35A does not expressly authorize the Clerk to order a person who has applied to be appointed or has been nominated as the guardian of a ward to produce his or her own financial or medical records or to submit to or cooperate with an assessment or evaluation regarding his or her suitability for appointment as the ward's guardian. However, if a prospective guardian fails to submit such evidence as the Clerk deems necessary to determine whether the prospective guardian should be appointed as the ward's guardian, the Clerk, in the sound exercise of the Clerk's discretion, may refuse to appoint the prospective guardian as the ward's guardian.

Factors that should be considered in appointing a guardian. In determining whether a particular person, corporation, agency, or official should be appointed as the guardian of an incapacitated adult, the Clerk should consider whether the prospective guardian

- is qualified to serve as the adult's guardian (*see* § 7.5 of this chapter);

- is willing to serve as the adult's guardian;

- is able to serve as the adult's guardian;

- understands the legal powers, duties, and responsibilities of a guardian;

- will act in the ward's best interest;

- will act in a fiduciary manner with respect to the ward and the ward's property;

- has a personal, private, or official interest that conflicts or may conflict with the ward's interests or that may hinder or be adverse to the discharge of the guardian's responsibilities;

- has been convicted of a felony;

- has wasted or mismanaged the property of the ward or others;

- has served in a fiduciary capacity with respect to the ward or others;

- has violated his or her fiduciary obligations to the ward or others;

- has been adjudicated incompetent;

- has engaged in any activity that would raise doubts regarding his or her honesty or integrity.

7.5
Qualifications and Disqualifications for Appointment of Guardians

A. Qualifications of Guardians

The Clerk may appoint an adult individual, a corporation, a disinterested public agent, or a public guardian as the general guardian, guardian of the person, or guardian of the estate of an incapacitated adult unless the individual, corporation, disinterested public agent, or public guardian is not legally qualified to serve as the respondent's guardian under G.S. Ch. 35A. G.S. 35A-1213(a).

B. Recommendation of Potential Guardians

The petitioner or applicant in an adult guardianship proceeding may submit for the Clerk's consideration the name or names of individuals, corporations, agencies, or officials as potential guardians for an incapacitated adult. G.S. 35A-1213(a). The Clerk also may consider guardianship recommendations made by the respondent's next of kin, the respondent, the respondent's attorney or *guardian ad litem*, or other persons. G.S. 35A-1213(a).

C. Limitations and Disqualifications

The Clerk may not appoint an adult individual or corporation as the guardian of an incapacitated adult unless the individual or corporation is willing to serve as the adult's guardian.

The Clerk may not appoint a corporation as the general guardian, guardian of the person, or guardian of the estate of an incapacitated adult unless the corporation's charter authorizes it to serve as a guardian or in a similar fiduciary capacity. G.S. 35A-1213(c).

An adult who is not a resident of North Carolina may be appointed as the general guardian, guardian of the person, or guardian of the estate of an incapacitated adult. A guardian who is not a resident of North Carolina, however, must indicate in writing his or her willingness to submit to the jurisdiction of North Carolina's courts in matters relating to his or her service as a guardian and must appoint a resident agent to accept service of process for the guardian in all actions or proceedings with respect to the guardianship. G.S. 35A-1213(b).

An employee of a mental health treatment facility (as defined in G.S. 122C-3(14)) may not be appointed as the guardian of an incapacitated adult who is an inpatient in or resident of the facility in which the employee works. G.S. 35A-1213(e).

Practice note: This provision applies only to persons who are employed by mental health treatment facilities. It does not apply to persons who are employed by nursing homes, adult care homes, or other treatment facilities that are not mental health facilities.

A person may not be appointed as the guardian of an incapacitated adult if the person has been adjudicated incompetent and his or her competency has not been restored. *See* G.S. 35A-1290(c)(1).

7.6
Statutory Priorities and Preferences Governing Appointment of Guardians

The Clerk generally must appoint a guardian for an incapacitated adult according to the following order of priority:

1. a qualified, willing, able, and suitable individual or corporation who has been nominated as general guardian, guardian of the person, or guardian of the estate by a valid, unrevoked durable power of attorney executed by an adult who has subsequently become incapacitated (G.S. 32A-10(b));

2. a qualified, willing, able, and suitable individual who has been nominated as guardian of the person by a valid, unrevoked health care power of attorney executed by an adult who has subsequently become incapacitated (G.S. 32A-22(b));

3. a qualified, willing, able, and suitable individual recommended as guardian pursuant to G.S. 35A-1212.1 by the last will and testament of the parent of an unmarried adult child;

4. any other qualified, willing, able, and suitable adult (G.S. 35A-1214);

5. a qualified, willing, able, and suitable corporation (including for-profit corporations, corporate financial institutions, and non-profit corporations) (G.S. 35A-1214);

6. a disinterested public agent (G.S. 35A-1214, discussed in § 7.7 of this chapter) or the public guardian (G.S. 35A-1270, discussed in § 7.8 of this chapter).

Nomination of guardian under the ward's power of attorney. The nomination of a guardian pursuant to G.S. 32A-10(b) or G.S. 32A-22(b) is not binding on the Clerk if the Clerk determines that there is good cause to appoint a different guardian.

Nomination of guardian under the last will and testament of the ward's parent. The recommendation of a guardian pursuant to G.S. 35A-1212.1 is not binding on the Clerk if the Clerk determines that appointing a different guardian is in the ward's best interest. G.S. 35A-1212.1.

No statutory priority for spouse or next of kin. Unlike the Uniform Guardianship and Protective Proceedings Act and North Carolina's law governing the administration of decedents' estates (G.S. 28A-4-1), G.S. Ch. 35A does not establish an order governing the preference or priority of an incapacitated adult's spouse, child, parent, sibling, or other relative to serve as the adult's guardian. Thus, the spouse, child, or parent of an incapacitated adult is not *per se* entitled to preference or priority as the adult's guardian *vis a vis* a qualified, willing, able, and suitable adult who is not related to the adult.

Limitations on appointment of disinterested public agent as guardian. A disinterested public agent may not be appointed as the guardian of an incapacitated adult unless there has been a diligent effort to find a qualified, willing, able, suitable, and appropriate individual or corporation to serve as the ward's guardian and the Clerk determines that appointing a disinterested public agent, rather than an individual or corporation, as guardian is in the ward's best interest. G.S. 35A-1214.

The appointment of a disinterested public agent as guardian is discussed in more detail in the following section of this chapter.

7.7
Appointment of Disinterested Public Agent Guardians

A. Definition of Disinterested Public Agent

A "disinterested public agent" is

- the director or assistant director of a local human services (social services, public health, mental health, aging, etc.) agency; *or*
- an officer, agent, or employee of a state human services agency. G.S. 35A-1202(4).

B. Appointment of Disinterested Public Agent as Guardian

Unless disqualified under G.S. 35A-1213(e) (*see* § 7.5C of this chapter), a disinterested public agent may be appointed by the Clerk as the general guardian, guardian of the person, or guardian of the estate of an incapacitated adult, and must serve as the adult's guardian if the Clerk orders him or her to do so. *See* G.S. 35A-1213(d).

Practice Note: Some state and local human services agencies have developed memoranda of understanding among themselves and the Clerk regarding the criteria and procedures for appointing disinterested public agents as guardians for incapacitated adults.

A disinterested public agent, however, may not be appointed as the guardian of an incapacitated adult unless there has been a diligent effort to find a qualified, willing, able, suitable, and appropriate individual or corporation to serve as the ward's guardian and the Clerk determines that appointing a disinterested public agent, rather than an individual or corporation, as guardian is in the ward's best interest. G.S. 35A-1214.

A disinterested public agent who is appointed as the guardian of an incapacitated adult serves in that capacity by virtue of his or her office or employment, which must be identified in the Clerk's order and in the letters of appointment issued by the Clerk. *See* G.S. 35A-1213(d). When a disinterested public agent's office or employment terminates, his or her successor in office or employment (or his or her immediate supervisor if there is no successor) succeeds him or her as guardian without further proceedings or appointment unless the Clerk orders otherwise. *See* G.S. 35A-1213(d).

C. Conflicts of Interest

Except as provided in G.S. 35A-1213(e) (*see* § 7.5C of this chapter), the fact that a disinterested public agent is employed by a state or local human services agency that provides financial assistance, services, or treatment to an incapacitated adult does not disqualify the disinterested public agent from being appointed or serving as the adult's guardian. *See* G.S. 35A-1202(4).

A disinterested public agent, however, may, at the time of his or her proposed appointment as guardian or at any time subsequent to his or her appointment as guardian, request the Clerk to appoint a different guardian if he or she believes that his or her role or the role of his or her agency in relation to the ward is such that his or her appointment or service as guardian would constitute a conflict of interest or believes there is any other reason that his or her appointment or service as guardian would not be in the ward's best interest. *See* G.S. 35A-1213(d).

D. DHHS Requirements Regarding Public Guardianship

Disinterested public agents who are appointed as guardians must meet guardianship training requirements established by the state Department of Health and Human Services (DHHS) and comply with DHHS rules governing the guardianship responsibilities of disinterested public agents. *See* G.S. 35A-1216.

E. Payment for Public Guardianship Services

A disinterested public agent who serves as the guardian of the estate of an incapacitated adult may be paid a commission from the adult's estate pursuant to G.S. 35A-1269. A disinterested public agent who serves as the guardian of the person of an incapacitated adult may be reimbursed from the ward's estate for reasonable and proper expenditures incurred in the performance of his or her duties as guardian. *See* G.S. 35A-1241(b).

Although guardianship services provided by a disinterested public agent may be paid from any public funding that is available to the state or local human services agency for guardianship services, little or no federal or state human services funding is expressly designated for guardianship services.

7.8
Appointment of Public Guardians

G.S. 35A-1270 authorizes, but does not require, the Clerk of Superior Court to appoint for a term of eight years a person as the public guardian for the county.

Bond. The public guardian must post a bond in accordance with G.S. 35A-1271.

Powers and duties. A public guardian who is appointed as the general guardian, guardian of the person, or guardian of the estate of an incapacitated adult has the same statutory powers and duties as other guardians of incapacitated adults. G.S. 35A-1272.

Compensation. A public guardian who is appointed as the general guardian, guardian of the person, or guardian of the estate of an incapacitated adult is entitled to the same compensation as other guardians of incapacitated adults. G.S. 35A-1272.

Letters of appointment. The public guardian appointed pursuant to G.S. 35A-1270 may be appointed by the Clerk as the general guardian or guardian of the estate of an incapacitated adult if the incapacitated adult does not have a general guardian or guardian of the estate and a period of six months has elapsed from the discovery of any property belonging to the incapacitated adult. G.S. 35A-1273(1).

The public guardian appointed pursuant to G.S. 35A-1270 also may be appointed by the Clerk as the general guardian or guardian of the estate or as the guardian of the person of an incapacitated adult if any person who is entitled to letters of guardianship files a written request that the Clerk issue letters of appointment to the public guardian. G.S. 35A-1273(2). If letters of appointment are issued to the public guardian under G.S. 35A-1273(2), the Clerk may, for sufficient cause, revoke the letters in response to the written application of any person who is entitled to qualify as the adult's guardian.

7.9
Order and Letters of Appointment

A. Order Appointing a Guardian

When appointing a guardian, the Clerk must enter an order setting forth:

- the nature of the guardianship or guardianships to be created;
- the name of the person or entity appointed as guardian with respect to each guardianship created; and
- the powers and duties of the guardian or guardians which, unless otherwise ordered by the Clerk, shall include the applicable statutory powers and duties set forth in Articles 8 and 9 of G.S. Chapter 35A. G.S. 35A-1215(a).

If the Clerk designates a human services agency to receive guardianship status reports pursuant to G.S. 35A-1242 and G.S. 35A-1243, the Clerk's guardianship order must identify the designated agency. G.S. 35A-1215(a)(3).

If the Clerk enters a "limited guardianship" order pursuant to G.S. 35A-1212(a), the Clerk's order should include provisions specifying the legal rights and privileges that are retained by the ward as well as any necessary and appropriate limitations with respect to the guardian's powers. G.S. 35A-1215(b).

If a guardian is required to post a bond, the Clerk's order also may include provisions with respect to the amount, terms, and conditions of the guardian's bond.

B. Creation of Guardianship

The Clerk's guardianship order may create a guardianship of an incapacitated adult's person, a guardianship of an incapacitated adult's estate, or a general guardianship of the incapacitated adult's person and estate.

The Clerk should not create a general guardianship unless the Clerk determines that the adult needs a guardian who can serve as the guardian of the adult's person and estate. If an incapacitated adult does not have an estate but needs a guardian of his or her person, the Clerk generally should create only a guardianship of the incapacitated adult's person. If an incapacitated adult needs a guardian of his or her estate but does not need a guardian of his or her person, the Clerk should create only a guardianship of the incapacitated adult's estate and should not create a general guardianship or a guardianship of the adult's person.

C. Appointment of Guardians

If the Clerk determines that creation of a general guardianship is appropriate, the Clerk may appoint one person or entity as the adult's general guardian or may appoint one person or entity as the guardian of the adult's person and another person or entity as the guardian of the adult's estate.

D. Appointment of Co-Guardians

G.S. Chapter 35A neither expressly authorizes nor prohibits the Clerk from appointing two or more persons or entities to serve as co-guardians of an incapacitated adult, as co-guardians of an incapacitated adult's person, or as co-guardians of an incapacitated adult's estate. In practice, however, Clerks sometimes appoint two or more persons or entities to serve jointly as the co-guardians of an incapacitated adult. *See Parker v. Barefoot*, 61 N.C. App. 232 (1983) (adult son and daughter of an incapacitated adult were appointed as her co-guardians).

Practice Note: If the Clerk appoints two or more persons or entities as the co-guardians of an incapacitated adult, the Clerk's order should specify the manner in which the co-guardians will exercise their shared powers and duties. *See* G.S. 28A-13-6 (governing the exercise of powers by co-administrators or co-executors).

E. Letters of Appointment

Bond requirements. Before issuing letters of appointment to a general guardian or guardian of the estate of an incapacitated adult (other than a guardian appointed pursuant to a recommendation under G.S. 35A-1212.1 that includes a provision specifically directing that no bond be required), the Clerk must require the guardian to post a bond in accordance with Article 7 of G.S. Ch. 35A or other applicable law. G.S. 35A-1231(a). The Clerk may require a nonresident guardian of the person of an incapacitated adult to post a bond. G.S. 35A-1213(b).

Issuance of letters of appointment. After the Clerk has entered an order appointing a person or entity as the guardian of an incapacitated adult and the guardian has accepted appointment (unless the guardian is a disinterested public agent or the public guardian), posted a bond (if a bond is required), and taken an oath to faithfully and honestly discharge the guardian's duties according to law, the Clerk must issue letters of appointment to the guardian, under the Clerk's signature and official seal, evidencing the guardian's authority to act as the incapacitated adult's general guardian, guardian of the person, or guardian of the estate. G.S. 35A-1206.

Contents of letters of appointment. The letters of appointment issued to the guardian of an incapacitated adult should state the name of the incapacitated adult, the name of the incapacitated adult's guardian, the date the guardian qualified for issuance of the letters of appointment, and the date the letters of appointment were issued.

If the Clerk enters a limited guardianship order, the letters of appointment issued to the guardian should specify the legal rights that are retained by the incapacitated adult and the manner and extent to which the guardian's powers are limited.

CHAPTER 8:
Mediation of Adult Guardianship Cases

8.1
Statutory Authority and Rules

Except as otherwise provided in G.S. 7A-38.3B(b), G.S. 7A-38.3B allows the Clerk to order mandatory mediation of any matter that is within the Clerk's exclusive and original jurisdiction, including matters regarding the appointment of a guardian for an incapacitated adult pursuant to G.S. Chapter 35A.

G.S. 7A-38.3B specifies the procedures that govern the mediation of guardianship proceedings involving incapacitated adults. These statutory procedures are supplemented by rules adopted by the North Carolina Supreme Court governing the mediation of guardianship and other matters pending before the Clerk of Superior Court. These rules are available online: www.nccourts.org/Courts/CRS/Councils/DRC/Clerks/Rules.asp.

The following discussion is based on the requirements of G.S. 7A-38.3B and the Supreme Court rules governing mediation of matters before the Clerk.

8.2
Ordering Mediation in Adult Guardianship Cases

A. Clerk's Authority to Order Mediation

The Clerk *may*, on the Clerk's own initiative or in response to a motion requesting mediation filed by a party or other interested person, enter an order requiring mediation of some or all issues related to a proceeding seeking the appointment of a guardian for an incapacitated adult pursuant to G.S. Ch. 35A.

Practice Note: The Clerk is not required to hold a hearing to determine whether mandatory mediation should be ordered in a pending guardianship proceeding.

The decision whether to order mandatory mediation in a pending guardianship proceeding is vested in the Clerk's discretion.

Mandatory mediation of some or all of the issues regarding the guardianship of an allegedly incapacitated adult *may* be appropriate if the respondent or another party or interested person is contesting

- the petitioner's allegations regarding the respondent's incapacity;
- the nature and extent of the respondent's incapacity;
- whether the respondent needs a guardian;
- whether a plenary or limited guardianship is appropriate; or
- who should be appointed as the respondent's guardian.

Mandatory mediation of guardianship matters generally is *not* appropriate with respect to

- uncontested proceedings;
- matters involving only questions of law;
- matters requiring immediate judicial action (such as appointment of an interim guardian);
- cases involving alleged criminal activity or domestic abuse, elder abuse, or substance abuse by a party;
- cases in which a party exhibits volatile or hostile behavior; or
- cases in which the possibility of coercion or intimidation of a vulnerable party exists.

B. Order for Mandatory Mediation in Guardianship Proceedings

If the Clerk determines that mandatory mediation is appropriate with respect to a pending adult guardianship proceeding, the Clerk must enter an order, using form AOC-G-301T,

- requiring that a mediation be held with respect to some or all of the issues in the case;

- establishing a deadline for the selection of a mediator;

- establishing a deadline for completion of the mediation;

- stating the names of the persons and entities who must attend the mediation;

- stating the parties' right to select their own mediator;

- stating the rate of compensation that will be allowed if the parties fail to select a mediator and the mediator is appointed by the court; and

- informing the parties' of their responsibilities regarding payment of the mediator's fee.

Practice Note: An order requiring mediation of an adult guardianship proceeding does not delay other proceedings in the matter unless the Clerk orders otherwise.

C. Motion to Dispense with Mediation

If the Clerk has entered an order requiring mediation of an adult guardianship proceeding, any party, interested person, or fiduciary may file a motion asking the Clerk to dispense with mediation. The motion must state the reasons that relief is sought and be served on the mediator and on all persons who have been ordered to attend the mediation. The Clerk may grant the motion for good cause shown.

D. Voluntary Dismissal After Entry of Order for Mediation

In adult guardianship proceedings seeking an adjudication of a respondent's incapacity, the petitioner may not voluntarily dismiss the proceeding after the Clerk has entered an order requiring mediation.

8.3
Selecting the Mediator

Selection by agreement. The parties involved in an adult guardianship proceeding may select, by agreement, a mediator who has been certified by the Dispute Resolution Commission to mediate estate and guardianship matters.

If the parties select a mediator, the petitioner must file a notice (AOC-G-302T) with the Clerk within the time specified in the Clerk's order for mediation. The notice must state the name, address, and phone number of the mediator and the rate at which the mediator will be compensated.

Certification of mediators for estate and guardianship matters. Approximately 160 persons have been certified to mediate estate and guardianship matters. A listing of persons who have been

certified to mediate estate and guardianship matters is available online: http://www1.aoc.
state.nc.us/mediatorpublic/clerkmenu.do.

Designation of mediator by Clerk. If the parties in an adult guardianship proceeding fail to
agree regarding the selection of a mediator, the Clerk must appoint a mediator who has been
certified by the Dispute Resolution Commission to mediate estate and guardianship matters.
In making this appointment, the Clerk must, absent good cause, appoint qualified mediators
by rotation from a list of certified mediators within the jurisdiction without regard to the
mediator's occupation, race, gender, religion, natural origin, or disability, and without regard
to whether the mediator is an attorney.

Disqualification of mediator. Any person who has been ordered to attend a mediation may
move that a mediator who has been selected by the parties or appointed by the Clerk be
disqualified for cause from mediating the case. The Clerk may grant such a motion for good
cause shown.

8.4
Responsibilities of Respondent's Counsel or *Guardian ad Litem*

If the petitioner in an adult guardianship proceeding is represented by counsel, the attorney
who is retained by a respondent or appointed as the *guardian ad litem* for a respondent in an
adult guardianship proceeding and the petitioner's attorney must discuss with each other
as soon as practicable the means available to the parties to resolve their disputes through
mediation and other settlement procedures without resort to a contested hearing before the
Clerk. The respondent's attorney or *guardian ad litem* and petitioner's attorney also must
discuss with each other which neutral third party would best suit their clients and the matter
in controversy.

If the Clerk orders mandatory mediation of an adult guardianship proceeding, the
respondent's attorney or *guardian ad litem* must attend the mediation hearing and represent
the respondent's interests in the mediation.

8.5
The Mediation Process

A. Location of Mediation Hearings

The mediation may be held at any location agreed upon by the mediator and all of the
persons who have been ordered to attend the mediation. In the absence of such an agreement,
the mediator must notify the parties that the mediation will be held in the courthouse or
another public or community building in the county where the matter is pending.

B. Date and Time of Mediation Hearings

Scheduling. The mediator must try to schedule the mediation at a time that is convenient to all of the participants. In the absence of an agreement by the participants regarding the date and time of the mediation, the mediator shall select a date and time for the mediation.

Notice. The mediator must notify the parties of the date and time for the mediation and conduct the mediation before the date specified in the Clerk's order requiring mediation.

Extension and continuances. The mediator or any person ordered to participate in mediation may request the Clerk to extend the deadline for completion of mediation. The request to extend the deadline for completing the mediation must state the reasons therefor and be delivered to the mediator and all persons who have been ordered to participate in the mediation. The Clerk may grant the request without hearing by setting a new deadline for completion of the mediation. Notice of the Clerk's decision must be filed with the court and delivered by the person who made the request to the mediator and all persons who have been ordered to participate in the mediation.

The parties involved in the mediation of an adult guardianship proceeding and their attorneys must promptly notify the mediator of any significant problems they may have with the dates set for mediation sessions and must keep the mediator informed as to such problems as may arise before a scheduled mediation session.

After mediation has been scheduled for a specific date, a person ordered to participate in mediation may not unilaterally postpone the mediation. A mediator, however, may postpone a mediation session upon the request of a participant, notice to other participants, and a finding of good cause beyond the control of the moving party. A mediator also may postpone a scheduled mediation session with the consent of all of the participants.

Recesses. The mediator may recess the mediation at any time and may set the time for reconvening the mediation. Notice of the date and time for reconvening the mediation is not required if the time for reconvening the mediation is set before the mediation is recessed.

C. Attendance and Participation at Mediation Hearings

Persons required to attend and participate in mediation. The Clerk's order requiring mediation of an adult guardianship proceeding must specify the persons who are required to participate in mediation. The following persons, and their attorneys, may be ordered to attend and participate in the mediation of an adult guardianship proceeding:

- the named parties to the proceeding;
- other persons or entities who have a right, interest, or claim in the matter;
- the respondent's next of kin;
- other persons or entities that the Clerk deems necessary for resolution of the matter;
- other persons or entities identified by the Clerk as possessing useful information about the matter and whose attendance would be beneficial to the mediation;
- fiduciaries of named parties, interested persons, or nonparty participants.

All persons and entities who are ordered to attend and participate in mediation of an adult guardianship proceeding and the lawyers who represent those persons and entities must attend and participate in the mediation unless excused by the Clerk or by agreement of the mediator and all parties involved in the mediation.

Practice Note: The mediator may allow persons other than those specified in the Clerk's order to attend and participate in the mediation of an adult guardianship proceeding.

Sanctions for failure to attend or participate in mediation. The Clerk, after notice and hearing, may enter an order imposing sanctions on any person, entity, or lawyer who fails, without good cause, to attend and participate in the mediation of an adult guardianship proceeding as required by the Clerk's order. These sanctions may include an appropriate monetary sanction, including but not limited to, payment of fines, payment of attorney's fees, payment of mediator fees, and payment of expenses and loss of earnings incurred by persons attending the mediation. A person seeking sanctions against another person must do so in a written motion stating the grounds therefor and the relief sought. The Clerk also may initiate a sanction proceeding on the Clerk's own motion by entry of a show cause order.

D. Authority and Duties of Mediator

The mediator shall at all times be in control of the mediation and the procedures to be followed. The mediator's conduct must be in accordance with the standards of conduct for mediators promulgated by the North Carolina Supreme Court. The mediator must act impartially and advise all participants of any circumstances bearing on the mediator's possible bias, prejudice, or partiality.

Private communications. The mediator may communicate privately with any participant or counsel prior to, during, or after the mediation. The mediator, however, must disclose to all participants at the beginning of the mediation any prior private communications between the mediator and a participant or counsel. The mediator also must disclose to participants at the beginning of the mediation the circumstances under which the mediator may meet and communicate privately with participants or other persons and whether, or under what circumstances, communications with the mediator will be held in confidence.

E. Mediated Agreements

No one participating in the mediation of an adult guardianship proceeding is required to make a settlement offer or demand that is contrary to the participant's best interests.

If an agreement is reached upon some or all of the issues involved in the mediation of an adult guardianship proceeding, the participants must reduce its terms to writing and sign the agreement along with their counsel. These agreements must include the following language in a prominent place in the document: "This agreement is not binding on the Clerk but will be presented to the Clerk as an aid to reaching a just resolution of the matter."

F. Impasse in Mediation

The mediator has a continuing duty to determine whether an impasse exists. To that end, the mediator must inquire of and consider the desires of the participants to cease or continue the mediation. If the mediator determines that an impasse exists, the mediator must terminate the mediation.

G. Reporting the Results of Mediation

The mediator must file a report (AOC-G-303T) with the Clerk within five days of completion of the mediation stating whether the mediation resulted in a proposed settlement or an impasse. If the participants reached an agreement, the mediator's report must include a copy of the agreement.

The mediator's report must include a report of the time spent by the mediator in connection with the mediation and the fees charged for mediation.

8.6
Consideration of Mediated Agreements by the Clerk

An agreement or settlement reached by the parties in the mediation of an adult guardianship proceeding is not binding on the Clerk or on the parties. The agreement, however, may be offered into evidence at the hearing of an adult guardianship matter and may be considered by the Clerk for the purpose of reaching a just and fair resolution of the matter.

Evidence of statements made and conduct occurring in the mediation of an adult guardianship proceeding in which an agreement is reached is admissible in a hearing before the Clerk in the pending proceeding. G.S. 7A-38.3B(g)(3).

Practice Note: Evidence of statements made and conduct occurring in the mediation of an adult guardianship proceeding is *not* admissible in a hearing before the Clerk in the pending proceeding if the mediation results in an impasse.

8.7
Cost of Mediation

When a mediator is selected by the parties, the mediator's compensation is determined by an agreement between the mediator and the parties.

When a mediator is appointed by the Clerk, the mediator's compensation is determined by the Supreme Court's rules governing mediation of matters before the Clerk.

In mediations involving adult guardianship proceedings, the mediator's fee must be paid by the participants in shares as determined by the Clerk. The Clerk, however, may not require a person to pay a share of the mediator's fee if the Clerk determines that the person is indigent. Nor may the Clerk assess a share of the mediator's fee against the estate of an incapacitated adult, a fiduciary, or an interested person unless the Clerk enters an order making specific written findings of fact justifying the taxing of costs.

CHAPTER 9:
Appeal of Guardianship Orders

9.1
Appeal of Final and Interlocutory Orders

Appeal of final orders. A final order entered by the Clerk regarding the incapacity of a respondent in an adult guardianship proceeding or the appointment of a guardian for an incapacitated respondent may be appealed to the Superior Court. G.S. 35A-1115; G.S. 1-301.2(e); G.S. 1-301.2(g)(1); G.S. 1-301.3(c).

Review of interlocutory orders on appeal. Upon an appeal from a final order entered by the Clerk in an adult guardianship proceeding, the Superior Court may review any intermediate or interlocutory order entered by the Clerk in the proceeding if the order involves the merits of the proceeding and necessarily affects the Clerk's judgment therein and the appellant's objection thereto has been properly preserved. G.S. 1-278.

Immediate appeal of interlocutory orders. Interlocutory orders entered by the Clerk in adult guardianship proceedings are immediately appealable and subject to review by the Superior Court only if they affect a substantial right of a party that cannot be adequately protected by timely appeal from the Clerk's ultimate disposition of the proceeding. *See In re Watson*, 70 N.C. App. 120, 123 (1984).

9.2
Standing to Appeal

A. "Aggrieved" Party

A party who is "aggrieved" by a final order entered by the Clerk in an adult guardianship proceeding has standing to appeal that order to the Superior Court. G.S. 35A-1115; G.S. 1-301.2(e); G.S. 1-301.2(g)(1); G.S. 1-301.3(c).

A party is aggrieved by a final order in an adult guardianship proceeding if the order directly, substantially, and injuriously affects the party's legal rights. *See Culton v. Culton*, 327 N.C. 624, 625–626 (1990).

B. Appeal by Respondent

Because an order determining that a respondent is incapacitated and appointing a guardian for the respondent directly and substantially affects the respondent's legal rights, it is clear that the respondent, or the respondent's attorney or *guardian ad litem* acting on behalf of the respondent, has standing to appeal the final order of the Clerk in an adult guardianship proceeding. It is also clear that the respondent, or the respondent's attorney or *guardian ad litem* acting on behalf of the respondent, has standing to appeal an order by the Clerk denying the respondent's motion for restoration of competency. *See* G.S. 35A-1130(f).

C. Appeal by Petitioner

It is less clear whether a petitioner or applicant is "aggrieved" by and may appeal a final order determining that a respondent is not incapacitated or appointing someone other than the petitioner, the applicant, or a person recommended by the petitioner or applicant.

D. Appeal by "Interested Persons" and Next of Kin

A person who is an "interested person" or the respondent's next of kin does not have standing to appeal a final order regarding the respondent's incapacity or guardianship unless that person has been made a party to the proceeding. *See In re Ward*, 337 N.C. 443 (1994); *Siler v. Blake*, 20 N.C. 90 (1838).

9.3
Notice of Appeal

Written notice of appeal from the Clerk's final order in an adult guardianship proceeding must be given within 10 days from the date on which the order was reduced to writing, signed by the Clerk, and filed with the Clerk. G.S. 1-301.2(e); G.S. 1-301.3(c). *See also* N.C. R. Civ. P. Rule 58(a) (governing entry of judgments).

The appellant must file the notice of appeal with the Clerk and serve it on the other parties to the proceeding. G.S. 1-301.2(e); G.S. 1-301.3(c).

The notice of appeal must specify the basis for the appeal. G.S. 1-301.3(c).

9.4
Stay Pending Appeal

The appeal of an order by the Clerk finding a respondent incapacitated does *not* stay the appointment of a guardian for the respondent unless the Superior Court or the North Carolina Court of Appeals so orders. G.S. 35A-1115.

The Clerk or a superior court judge may stay an order by the Clerk appointing a guardian for an incapacitated adult upon the appellant's posting an appropriate bond set by the Clerk or judge. G.S. 1-301.3(c).

Unless otherwise ordered by a superior court judge, the Clerk retains authority to enter orders affecting an adult guardianship during the pendency of an appeal of the Clerk's guardianship order to the superior court. G.S. 1-301.3(c).

9.5
Appellate Jurisdiction of the Superior Court

Practice Note: The law, procedures, and standard of review for the Superior Court's appellate review of adult guardianship cases depend on whether the appeal involves only issues regarding the respondent's incapacity, only other issues regarding the appointment of a guardian for the respondent, or both. *See* G.S. 35A-1115; G.S. 1-301.2; G.S. 1-301.3.

A. Appeals Involving Incapacity

An appeal from the Clerk's order regarding a respondent's incapacity is heard and determined by the Superior Court *de novo*. G.S. 35A-1115.

B. Appeals Involving Guardianship

An appeal from the Clerk's order appointing a guardian for an incapacitated adult or from other orders arising in connection with an adult guardianship is not heard and determined by the superior court *de novo*. Appeals in these matters generally are reviewed by the superior court "on the record." G.S. 1-301.3(d).

The superior court's appellate jurisdiction with respect to these appeals is limited to determining

- whether the findings of fact included in the Clerk's order are supported by the evidence in the record;

- whether the Clerk's conclusions of law are supported by the Clerk's findings of fact; and

- whether the Clerk's order is consistent with the Clerk's conclusions of law and with applicable law. G.S. 1-301.3(d).

9.6
Appellate Procedure in Superior Court

A. Appeals Involving Incapacity

De novo hearing. In a *de novo* appeal regarding a respondent's incapacity, the superior court should follow procedures similar to those described in Chapter 5 of this manual. Following the *de novo* hearing, the superior court judge must enter an order determining whether or to what extent the respondent is incapacitated.

Dismissal. If the judge (or jury) determines that the respondent is not incapacitated, the judge must dismiss the case.

Remand or review of guardianship. If the judge (or jury) determines that the respondent is incapacitated, the judge must remand the case to the Clerk for further proceedings or, if the Clerk's order appointing a guardian for the respondent has been appealed, review the Clerk's guardianship order pursuant to G.S. 1-301.3(d).

B. Appeals Involving Guardianship

Transcript or summary of evidence. With respect to appeals that are not heard *de novo*, a transcript of the proceedings before the Clerk may be ordered by any party, by the Clerk, or by the presiding judge. G.S. 1-301.3(f). If an adult guardianship proceeding was not recorded, the Clerk must submit to the superior court a summary of the evidence presented to the Clerk. G.S. 1-301.3(f).

Receiving additional evidence. If the superior court judge determines that the record is insufficient with respect to an evidentiary issue, the judge may receive additional evidence on that issue and, if the judge chooses to do so, may continue the case if necessary to allow the parties time to prepare for a hearing to receive additional evidence. G.S. 1-301.3(f).

Evidentiary errors. If the judge finds prejudicial error in the admission or exclusion of evidence, the judge may either remand the matter to the Clerk for hearing or determine the appeal on the basis of the record. G.S. 1-301.3(d).

Standard of review, remand, or affirmance. If the judge determines that the Clerk's findings of fact are not supported by the evidence, that the Clerk's conclusions of law are not supported by the findings, that the Clerk's order is not consistent with the Clerk's conclusions of law, or that the Clerk's order is not consistent with applicable law, the judge must remand the case to the Clerk for such further action as is necessary with respect to the guardianship matter. G.S. 1-301.3(e).

If, in an appeal that is not heard *de novo*, the judge determines that the Clerk's findings of fact are supported by the evidence, that the Clerk's conclusions of law are supported by the findings, that the Clerk's order is consistent with the Clerk's conclusions of law, and that the Clerk's order is consistent with applicable law, the judge must enter an order affirming the Clerk's order.

Superior court judge may not appoint guardian. A superior court judge who has heard an appeal regarding an adult guardianship matter may not appoint a person or entity as the respondent's guardian or enter any order, other than an order affirming the Clerk's order or remanding the matter for further proceedings before the Clerk, that affects guardianship matters that are within the Clerk's original and exclusive jurisdiction. *See In re Simmons*, 266 N.C. 702 (1966).

9.7
Appellate Review by the Court of Appeals and Supreme Court

A party who is aggrieved by a final order or judgment entered by a superior court judge in an adult guardianship proceeding may appeal the order or judgment to the North Carolina Court of Appeals. *See* G.S. 1-277; G.S. 7A-27(e). The North Carolina Rules of Appellate Procedure govern the appeal of adult guardianship cases to the North Carolina Court of Appeals and the North Carolina Supreme Court.

9.8
Abatement of Appeal

The death of the respondent in an adult guardianship proceeding during the pendency of an appeal to the superior court, the North Carolina Court of Appeals, or the North Carolina Supreme Court abates the appeal. *See In re Higgins*, 160 N.C. App. 704 (2003).

CHAPTER 10:
Modification and Termination of Guardianship Orders

10.1
Termination of Guardianship

The guardianship of an incapacitated adult is terminated

- upon death of the incapacitated adult (G.S. 35A-1295(a)(3)); or

- upon the entry of an order restoring the ward's competency pursuant to G.S. 35A-1130 (G.S. 35A-1295(a)(2)).

Except as otherwise provided by G.S. 35A-1295(b), G.S. 35A-1266, or other law, the powers and duties of a guardian with respect to the person and property of an incapacitated adult terminate upon termination of the guardianship. G.S. 35A-1295(a).

Within 60 days after a guardianship is terminated pursuant to G.S. 35A-1295, the guardian must file a final account with the Clerk. G.S. 35A-1266. After the Clerk approves the guardian's final account, the Clerk must enter an order discharging the guardian from further liability. G.S. 35A-1266.

10.2
Restoration of Competency

A. Motion for Restoration of Competency

The guardian of an incapacitated adult, the incapacitated adult for whom a guardian has been appointed, or any "interested person" may petition the Clerk to restore an incapacitated adult's competency by filing a verified motion in the cause with the Clerk who is exercising jurisdiction with respect to the incapacitated adult's guardianship. G.S. 35A-1130(a).

A motion seeking restoration of an incapacitated adult's competency must set forth facts tending to show that the adult has sufficient capacity to manage his or her own affairs and to make and communicate important decisions regarding his or her person, family, and property. G.S. 35A-1130(a); G.S. 35A-1101(7).

The movant must serve a copy of the motion on the ward, the ward's guardian, and any other parties to the guardianship proceeding pursuant to Rule 4 of the N.C. Rules of Civil Procedure. G.S. 35A-1130(b).

B. Right to Counsel and Appointment of Attorney as *Guardian ad Litem*

The ward is entitled to retain counsel, if he or she is capable of doing so, and to be represented by retained counsel in a proceeding seeking restoration of the ward's competency. G.S. 35A-1130(c).

If the ward is indigent and is not represented by counsel, an attorney must be appointed in accordance with rules adopted by the N.C. Indigent Defense Services Commission to represent the ward as the ward's *guardian ad litem*. G.S. 35A-1130(c). The attorney who was appointed as an incapacitated adult's *guardian ad litem* pursuant to G.S. 35A-1107 in the proceeding to appoint a guardian for the incapacitated adult does not, by virtue of that fact alone, serve as the ward's attorney or *guardian ad litem* in a proceeding seeking restoration of the ward's competency under G.S. 35A-1130; however, the Clerk will often reappoint the attorney who was previously appointed as the incapacitated adult's *guardian ad litem* to serve in that capacity in a proceeding seeking restoration of competency.

If the ward is not indigent and is not represented by counsel and the Clerk determines that the ward's interests are not adequately represented by the ward's guardian, the Clerk may appoint a *guardian ad litem* pursuant to Rule 17 of the N.C. Rules of Civil Procedure to represent the ward's interests in a proceeding seeking restoration of the ward's competency. However, an attorney or other person who is appointed as a ward's *guardian ad litem* for a nonindigent ward in a proceeding under G.S. 35A-1130 is appointed pursuant to Rule 17 of the N.C. Rules of Civil Procedure, *not* G.S. 35A-1130(c) and the rules adopted by the N.C. Indigent Defense Services Commission, and therefore is *not* entitled to compensation from the N.C. Office of Indigent Defense Services.

C. Hearing, Multidisciplinary Evaluation, and Right to Jury Trial

Upon the filing of a motion seeking restoration of an incapacitated adult's competency, the Clerk must set a date, time, and place for a hearing regarding the ward's capacity. G.S. 35A-1130(b).

Absent good cause, the hearing must be held not less than 10 days and not more than 30 days from the date of service of the motion and notice of hearing on the ward or the ward's guardian. G.S. 35A-1130(b).

Upon motion of any party or on the Clerk's own motion, the Clerk may order a multidisciplinary evaluation regarding the ward's capacity. G.S. 35A-1130(c). Multidisciplinary evaluations are discussed in more detail in Chapters 5 and 6 of this manual.

The ward, upon request of the ward, the ward's *guardian ad litem*, or the ward's counsel, is entitled to a jury trial on the issue of the ward's capacity. G.S. 35A-1130(c). The Clerk may order, on the Clerk's own motion, a jury trial on the issue of the ward's capacity in accordance with Rule 39(b) of the N.C. Rules of Civil Procedure. G.S. 35A-1130(c). The jury in a proceeding seeking restoration of a ward's capacity consists of 6, not 12, persons selected in accordance with G.S. Chapter 9. G.S. 35A-1130(c).

D. Standard and Burden of Proof

A ward's competency must be restored if the Clerk or jury finds, by a preponderance of the evidence, that the ward has sufficient capacity to manage his or her own affairs and to make and communicate important decisions regarding his or her person, family, and property. G.S. 35A-1130(d); G.S. 35A-1101(7).

E. Order and Appeal

If the Clerk or jury finds that the ward has sufficient capacity to manage his or her own affairs and to make and communicate important decisions regarding his or her person, family, and property, the Clerk must enter an order adjudicating that the ward is restored to competency. G.S. 35A-1130(d). Upon entry of an order restoring a ward's competency, the ward has the right to manage his or her affairs, make contracts, control and sell his or her property, and exercise his or her other legal rights as if he or she had never been adjudicated incompetent. G.S. 35A-1130(d). Following entry of an order restoring a ward's competency, the ward's guardian must file a final account with the Clerk pursuant to G.S. 35A-1266. G.S. 35A-1130(e). After the Clerk approves the guardian's final account, the Clerk must enter an order discharging the guardian from further liability. G.S. 35A-1130(e); G.S. 35A-1266.

If the Clerk or jury finds that there is insufficient evidence that the ward has sufficient capacity to manage his or her own affairs and to make and communicate important decisions regarding his or her person, family, and property, the Clerk must enter an order denying the motion. G.S. 35A-1130(f). The ward may appeal the Clerk's order denying a motion seeking restoration of the ward's competency to superior court for trial *de novo*. G.S. 35A-1130(f); G.S. 1-301.2.

G.S. 35A-1116 appears to govern the taxing of costs and fees in proceedings seeking the restoration of a ward's competency. The payment of costs and fees under G.S. 35A-1116 is discussed in Chapter 5 of this manual.

10.3
Modification of Guardianship Orders

Any "interested person" may file a motion in the cause with the Clerk in the county in which an adult guardianship is docketed requesting modification of the guardianship order or consideration of any other matter pertaining to the guardianship that is within the Clerk's jurisdiction. G.S. 35A-1207(a); G.S. 35A-1203. *See also* G.S. 35A-1290 (authorizing the Clerk, upon "information or complaint," to enter orders for the better management of the estates, the better care and maintenance of wards and their dependents, and the protection of the interests of wards).

Unless otherwise ordered by the Clerk, a motion under G.S. 35A-1207(a) and notice of hearing on the motion must be served by the movant pursuant to Rule 5 of the N.C. Rules of Civil Procedure on all parties to the guardianship proceeding and on such other persons as the Clerk may direct. G.S. 35A-1207(c). If the Clerk finds reasonable cause to believe that an emergency exists that threatens the physical well-being of the ward or constitutes a risk of substantial injury to the ward's estate, the Clerk may enter an appropriate *ex parte* order to address the emergency pending the disposition of the matter at the hearing. G.S. 35A-1207(d).

Appointment of Guardian ad Litem. G.S. Chapter 35A does not specifically address the appointment of an attorney to represent an incapacitated adult in a proceeding to modify a guardianship under G.S. 35A-1207. The attorney who was appointed as an incapacitated adult's *guardian ad litem* pursuant to G.S. 35A-1107 in the proceeding to appoint a guardian for the incapacitated adult does not, by virtue of that fact alone, serve as the ward's attorney or *guardian ad litem* in a guardianship proceeding under G.S. 35A-1207.

If the Clerk determines that the ward's interests are not adequately represented by the ward's guardian, the Clerk may appoint a *guardian ad litem* pursuant to Rule 17 of the N.C. Rules of Civil Procedure to represent the ward's interests in a guardianship proceeding under G.S. 35A-1207.

Practice Note: The N.C. Office of Indigent Defense Services has taken the position that it will compensate an attorney who is appointed as the ward's *guardian ad litem* in a proceeding under G.S. 35A-1207 if the ward is indigent because the issues are sufficiently related to the purposes of the original guardianship proceeding and appointment of a guardian.

10.4
Removal of Guardian

G.S. 35A-1290 authorizes the Clerk, upon "information or complaint," to remove the guardian of an incapacitated adult if the guardian

- mismanages the ward's estate;

- wastes or converts the ward's money or estate;

- neglects to care for or maintain the ward or the ward's dependents in a suitable manner;

- violates his or her fiduciary duties through default or misconduct;

- has a private interest that might tend to hinder or be adverse to carrying out the guardian's duties (*see also In re Armfield*, 113 N.C. App. 467 (1994));

- was originally unqualified for appointment as guardian and continues to be unqualified;

- is adjudicated incompetent;

- is convicted of a felony and the guardian's citizenship is not restored;

- is the spouse of the ward and has lost his or her spousal rights as provided in G.S. Chapter 31A;

- is likely to become insolvent or has sureties who are likely to become insolvent;

- no longer qualifies to serve as the ward's guardian;

- fails to post, renew, or increase a bond as required by law or court order;

- refuses or fails without justification to obey any process served on the guardian in connection with the guardianship;

- fails to file required accountings with the Clerk; or

- is unsuitable for any reason to continue serving as the ward's guardian (*see also In re Thomas*, ___ N.C. App. ___, 644 S.E.2d 608 (N.C. Ct. App. 2007) (authorizing the Clerk to remove a guardian and appoint a successor guardian for the "better care of the ward" without any finding of misconduct or unsuitability on the part of the incumbent guardian)).

G.S. 35A-1291 authorizes the Clerk to remove a guardian if the Clerk finds reasonable cause to believe that an emergency exists that threatens the physical well-being of the ward or constitutes a risk of substantial injury to the ward's estate. The language of this section implicitly suggests that the Clerk may not remove a guardian without a hearing in cases that do not involve an emergency that threatens the ward's physical well-being or constitutes a risk of substantial injury to the ward's estate. G.S. Chapter 35A, however, does not expressly state the procedures that the Clerk must follow in connection with a proceeding to remove a guardian under G.S. 35A-1290.

Emergency or interlocutory orders. If the Clerk revokes a guardian's letters of appointment pursuant to G.S. 35A-1290 or G.S. 35A-1291, the Clerk may enter such interlocutory orders and decrees as the Clerk finds necessary for the protection of the ward or the ward's estate pending the resolution of the matter and appointment of a successor guardian. G.S. 35A-1291.

Appointment of Guardian ad Litem. G.S. Chapter 35A does not specifically address the appointment of an attorney to represent an incapacitated adult in a proceeding to remove a guardian under G.S. 35A-1290. The attorney who was appointed as an incapacitated adult's *guardian ad litem* pursuant to G.S. 35A-1107 in the proceeding to appoint a guardian for the incapacitated adult does not, by virtue of that fact alone, serve as the ward's attorney or *guardian ad litem* in a proceeding to remove a guardian under G.S. 35A-1290.

If the Clerk determines that the ward's interests are not adequately represented by the ward's guardian, the Clerk may appoint a *guardian ad litem* pursuant to Rule 17 of the N.C. Rules of Civil Procedure to represent the ward's interests in a proceeding to remove a guardian under G.S. 35A-1290.

Practice Note: The N.C. Office of Indigent Defense Services has taken the position that it will compensate an attorney who is appointed as the ward's *guardian ad litem* in a proceeding under G.S. 35A-1290 if the ward is indigent because the issues are sufficiently related to the purposes of the original guardianship proceeding and appointment of a guardian.

Appointment of successor guardian. If the Clerk revokes a guardian's letters of appointment under G.S. 35A-1290 or G.S. 35A-1291, the Clerk must appoint a successor guardian. G.S. 35A-1293. The appointment of a successor guardian is discussed in § 10.6 of this chapter.

10.5
Resignation of Guardian

G.S. 35A-1292 allows the Clerk to accept the resignation of a guardian of an incapacitated adult. G.S. Chapter 35A, however, does not expressly state the procedures that the Clerk must follow in connection with the resignation of a guardian under G.S. 35A-1292.

Appointment of Guardian ad Litem. G.S. Chapter 35A does not specifically address the appointment of an attorney to represent an incapacitated adult in connection with the resignation of a guardian under G.S. 35A-1292. The attorney who was appointed as an incapacitated adult's *guardian ad litem* pursuant to G.S. 35A-1107 in the proceeding to appoint a guardian for the incapacitated adult does not, by virtue of that fact alone, serve as the ward's attorney or *guardian ad litem* in connection with the resignation of the ward's guardian under G.S. 35A-1292.

If the Clerk determines that the ward's interests are not adequately represented by the ward's guardian, the Clerk may appoint a *guardian ad litem* pursuant to Rule 17 of the N.C. Rules of Civil Procedure to represent the ward's interests in connection with the resignation of a ward's guardian under G.S. 35A-1292.

Practice Note: The N.C. Office of Indigent Defense Services has taken the position that it will compensate an attorney who is appointed as the ward's *guardian ad litem* in connection with the guardian's resignation under G.S. 35A-1292 if the ward is indigent because the issues are sufficiently related to the purposes of the original guardianship proceeding and appointment of a guardian.

Appointment of successor guardian. If the Clerk accepts a guardian's resignation under G.S. 35A-1292, the Clerk must appoint a successor guardian. G.S. 35A-1293. The appointment of a successor guardian is discussed in § 10.6 of this chapter.

10.6
Appointment of Successor Guardian

Upon the removal, death, or resignation of a guardian, the Clerk must appoint a successor guardian following the same criteria that would apply to the initial appointment of a guardian under Article 5 of G.S. Chapter 35A. G.S. 35A-1293.

Appointment of Guardian ad Litem. Although G.S. 35A-1293 requires the Clerk to "follow the same criteria that would apply to the initial appointment of a guardian" under Article 5 of G.S. Chapter 35A, G.S. 35A-1293 does not expressly require the Clerk, in appointing a successor guardian, to follow the *same procedures* that apply to the initial appointment of a guardian under Article 5 of G.S. Chapter 35A. It is not entirely clear, therefore, whether an attorney must be appointed pursuant to G.S. 35A-1107 to represent an incapacitated ward in connection with a proceeding involving the appointment of a successor guardian under G.S. 35A-1293. The attorney who was appointed as an incapacitated adult's *guardian ad litem* pursuant to G.S. 35A-1107 in the proceeding to appoint a guardian for the incapacitated adult probably does not, by virtue of that fact alone, serve as the ward's attorney or *guardian ad litem* in connection with the appointment of a successor guardian under G.S. 35A-1293.

The Clerk may appoint a *guardian ad litem* pursuant to Rule 17 of the N.C. Rules of Civil Procedure to represent the ward's interests in connection with the appointment of a successor guardian under G.S. 35A-1292.

Practice Note: The N.C. Office of Indigent Defense Services has taken the position that it will compensate an attorney who is appointed as the ward's *guardian ad litem* in connection with the appointment of a successor guardian if the ward is indigent because the issues are sufficiently related to the original guardianship proceeding and appointment of a guardian.

10.7
Other Guardianship Proceedings

The guardianship of an incapacitated adult may involve legal proceedings other than those discussed above and in the preceding chapters of this manual. These other guardianship proceedings may include:

- proceedings related to the guardian's bond (G.S. Ch. 35A, Art. 7);
- proceedings seeking the Clerk's approval of the guardian's consent to medical or other care or treatment of a ward (G.S. 35A-1241(a)(3));
- proceedings to compel status reports (G.S. 35A-1244);
- proceedings involving the sterilization of a mentally ill or developmentally disabled ward in cases of medical necessity (G.S. 35A-1245);
- proceedings seeking the Clerk's approval of specific matters involving administration of the ward's estate (G.S. 35A-1251);
- proceedings related to returns and accountings regarding a ward's estate (G.S. Ch. 35A, Art. 10);
- proceedings for the appointment of an ancillary guardian for a nonresident ward (G.S. 35A-1280);
- proceedings involving the sale, mortgage, exchange, or lease of the ward's estate (G.S. Ch. 35A, Art. 14);
- proceedings involving the mortgage or sale of property in which the ward has an interest as a joint tenant by the entireties (G.S. Ch. 35A, Art. 15);
- proceedings involving the advancement of surplus income to a ward's relatives (G.S. Ch. 35A, Art. 16);
- proceedings seeking the approval of a superior court judge for gifts from a ward's estate (G.S. Ch. 35A, Arts. 17 and 18);
- proceedings making a gift of a ward's life interest in a trust (G.S. Ch. 35A, Art. 19); and
- proceedings to revoke a ward's health care power of attorney (G.S. 32A-22(a)).

Appointment of Guardian ad Litem. G.S. Chapter 35A does not specifically address the appointment of an attorney to represent an incapacitated adult in connection with the proceedings listed above, except for sterilization proceedings under G.S. 35A-1245 (providing for appointment of an attorney in accordance with IDS rules). The attorney who was appointed as an incapacitated adult's *guardian ad litem* pursuant to G.S. 35A-1107 in the proceeding to appoint a guardian for the incapacitated adult does not, by virtue of that fact alone, serve as the ward's attorney or *guardian ad litem* in connection with the proceedings listed above.

If the Clerk determines that the ward's interests are not adequately represented by the ward's guardian, the Clerk may appoint a *guardian ad litem* pursuant to Rule 17 of the N.C. Rules of Civil Procedure to represent the ward's interests in connection with the proceedings listed above.

Practice Note: The N.C. Office of Indigent Defense Services has taken the position that an attorney who is appointed as a ward's *guardian ad litem* in connection with the proceedings listed (other than sterilization proceedings) is appointed pursuant to Rule 17 of the N.C. Rules of Civil Procedure, *not* G.S. 35A-1107, and therefore is *not* entitled to compensation from the N.C. Office of Indigent Defense Services for his or her service as the ward's *guardian ad litem*.